America, Through the Spectacles of an Oriental Diplomat

Anthem Travel Classics

America, Through the Spectacles of an Oriental Diplomat

WU TINGFANG

Introduction by Jonathan Spence

ANTHEM PRESS
LONDON · NEW YORK · DELHI

Anthem Press
An imprint of Wimbledon Publishing Company
www.anthempress.com

This edition first published in UK and USA 2007
by Anthem Press
75-76 Blackfriars Road, London SE1 8HA, UK
or PO Box 9779, London SW19 7ZG, UK
and
244 Madison Ave. #116, New York, NY 10016, USA

First published by Frederick A. Stokes Co: New York, 1914

Introduction © Jonathan Spence 2007

British Library Cataloguing in Publication Data
A catalogue record for this book is available from the British Library.

Library of Congress Cataloging in Publication Data
A catalog record for this book has been requested.

1 3 5 7 9 10 8 6 4 2

ISBN 1 84331 269 7 (Pbk)
ISBN-13 978 1 84331 269 7 (Pbk)

Printed in EU

Contents

List of Illustrations

Introduction
Jonathan Spence

From the early seventeenth century onwards, China was the main focus for hundreds of books and pamphlets written by Westerners. The authors of these works came from a wide variety of backgrounds: they were missionaries (both Catholic and Protestant), soldiers and sailors, diplomats, technical advisors, journalists, casual travelers and seasoned explorers. Some had lived in China for years or decades and were striving to recapture lived experience. Others, especially novelists, philosophers, playwrights, had never been and did not intend to go. A fictional China was good enough for them.

This Western fascination with China was not, however, matched by any complementary Chinese desire to come to intellectual grips with the West. Not until the early nineteenth century did a handful of Chinese scholars and officials start reading about European and American governance and society, in an attempt to develop new skills and institutions that might help them to deflect the growing pressures from the West. It was not until the 1870s that a few Chinese officials were sent by the ruling Qing dynasty to take up newly created diplomatic posts in Europe and the United States, and a few of these pioneers kept diaries or wrote brief accounts of the countries they had served in. By the dawn of the twentieth century, a few Chinese who had the language knowledge were emboldened to write of their experiences in English. The first of these men to publish was Yung Wing, raised near Macao, and brought over to the United States by protestant missionaries, who arranged for his education in New England secondary schools and at Yale University. Yung Wing's memoir, "My Life in China and America," written in fluent English, was published in New York in 1909. The book described, in considerable detail, his experiences as a new kind of citizen of the world, seeking to find an identity that could draw from the linkages between the two civilizations. Shortly after came Wu Tingfang, whose book reprinted here, "America through the Spectacles of an Oriental Diplomat," also written in confidently idiomatic English, was published in New York by the Frederick Stokes company in April 1914.

Wu's unusual life experiences had well prepared him for the difficult task of attempting a comparison between the American and the Chinese civilizations. Born in Singapore in 1842, in a Chinese merchant's family, Wu was taken back to China when he was three, and initially received a conventional Chinese education. But he was soon transferred to an excellent British school in Hong Kong, and after graduation was appointed to jobs as an interpreter, and to posts in the Hong Kong government. Deeply interested in the study and practice of law, Wu traveled to England for further study, read law in London, and was called to the bar in 1876, becoming a barrister, the first Chinese in history to hold such a position. After returning to Hong Kong a year later to mourn the death of his father, he was selected for service on the Legislative Council (again, as the first Chinese to serve in that body), but after a few years took service with China's most prominent governor-general Li Hongzhang, a pioneering modernizer. Li selected Wu to help him in the difficult negotiations after two wars, both of which China had lost disastrously – one in 1885 with France, and one in 1895 with Japan. This experience made Wu a natural choice to serve as the Qing dynasty's minister to the United States, and he served in Washington for two terms, from 1897–1902, and from 1907–9. In the United States he became a well-known figure, lecturing to large and enthusiastic audiences on Chinese history and the Dynasty's prospects for change, advising the Librarian of Congress on the formation of the Chinese collection, and helping to negotiate major loans with American financiers for the building of China's railroads. Recalled to China in 1910, Wu became a leading supporter of the revolutionary government that overthrew the Qing dynasty in 1911, and in 1912 he helped orchestrate the Qing emperor's abdication which ended the two millennia-long cycle of China's centralized imperial rule. From then on, until his death in 1922, just before his eightieth birthday, Wu remained active in the rough and tumble politics of the time, where his legal, diplomatic and language skills were sorely needed as China drifted into the era of warlordism.

It is against this dramatic background that we should read Wu's engaging book, written in Shanghai during 1913, before the First World War had erupted in Europe, and when China still seemed as if it might be able to make a peaceful transition to a viable democratic and constitutional system. The book thus represents a certain optimism on Wu's part, as he mulls over his experiences in the United States and compares his experiences there to what he sees as the more enduring value structures of China. Whether talking about women's fashions, the exclusion of Chinese laborers, the protocol of formal dinner parties, the promise of air travel, the dangers of the naval arms race, child-rearing customs, horse-racing, mixed marriages, theatrical performances, the ideal length of time for presidents to serve, the parallels between hunting and warfare, the separate schooling for "colored people" so visible in the United States, or his ideas about healthy diet, pure air, teetotalism, or the links between athletic success and vegetarianism, Wu is a genial guide. We may smile and shake our heads at many of his declamations, but he never loses the ability to entertain us, and leaves us nostalgic for his world of almost a century ago, when the telephone was a new and vital harbinger of social change, and the possibility that "a wicked man might throw a bomb" from an airplane was just a science-fiction fantasy.

– Jonathan Spence

Preface

Of all nations in the world, America is the most interesting to the Chinese. A handful of people left England to explore this country: gradually their number increased, and, in course of time, emigrants from other lands swelled the population. They were governed by officials from the home of the first settlers, but when it appeared to them that they were being treated unjustly, they rebelled and declared war against their rulers, the strongest nation on the face of the earth. After seven years of strenuous, perilous, and bloody warfare, during which thousands of lives were sacrificed on both sides, the younger race shook off the yoke of the older, and England was compelled to recognize the independence of the American States. Since then, in the comparatively short space of one hundred and thirty years, those revolutionists and their descendants have not only made the commonwealth the richest in the world, but have founded a nation whose word now carries weight with all the other great powers.

The territory at first occupied was not larger than one or two provinces of China, but by purchase, and in other ways, the commonwealth has gradually grown till now it extends from the Atlantic to the Pacific Ocean, from the north where ice is perpetual to the south where the sun is as hot as in equatorial Singapore. This young republic has already produced many men and women who are distinguished in the fields of literature, science, art and invention. There hosts of men, who in their youth were as poor as church mice, have, by dint of perseverance and business capacity, become multi-millionaires. There you may see the richest man in the world living a simple and abstemious life, without pomp and ostentation, daily walking in the streets unattended even by a servant. Many of them have so much money that they do not know what to do with it. Many foreign counts, dukes, and even princes have been captured by their wealthy and handsome daughters, some of whom have borne sons who have become high officers of state in foreign lands. There you find rich people who devote their time and wealth to charitable works, sometimes endowing libraries not only in their own land, but all over the world; there you will find lynching tolerated, or impossible of prevention; there one man may kill another, and by the wonderful process of law escape the extreme penalty of death; there you meet the people who are most favourably disposed toward the maintenance of peace, and who hold conferences and conventions with that object in view almost every year; there an American multi-millionaire devotes a great proportion of his time to the propaganda of peace, and at his own expense has built in a foreign country a palatial building to be used as a tribunal of peace.* Yet these people have waged war on behalf of other nationalities who they thought were being unjustly treated and when victorious they have not held on to the fruits of their victory without paying a reasonable price.** There the inhabitants are, as a rule, extremely patriotic, and in a recent foreign war many gave up their businesses and professions and volunteered for service in the army; one of her richest sons enlisted and equipped a whole regiment at his own expense, and took command of it. In that country all the citizens are heirs apparent to the throne, called the White House. A man may become the chief ruler for a few years, but after leaving the White House he reverts to private citizenship; if he is a lawyer he may practise and appear before a judge, whom he appointed while he was president. There a woman may become a lawyer and plead a case before a court of justice on behalf of a male client; there freedom of speech and criticism are allowed to the extreme limit, and people are liable to be annoyed by slanders and libels without much chance of obtaining satisfaction; there you will see women wearing "Merry Widow" hats who are not widows but spinsters, or married women whose husbands are very much alive, and the hats in many cases are as large as three feet in diameter;*** there you may travel by rail most comfortably on palace cars, and at night you may sleep on Pullman cars, to find in the morning that a young lady has been sleeping in the berth above your bed. The people are most ingenious in that they can float a company and water the stock without using a drop of fluid; there are bears and bulls in the Stock Exchange, but you do not see these animals fight, although they roar and yell loudly enough. It is certainly a most extraordinary country. The people are wonderful and are most interesting and instructive to the Chinese.

Such a race should certainly be very interesting to study. During my two missions to America, where I resided nearly eight years, repeated requests were made that I should write my observations and impressions of America. I did not feel justified in doing so for several reasons: first, I could not find time for such a task amidst my official duties; secondly, although I had been travelling through many sections of the country, and had come in contact officially and socially with many classes of people, still there might be some features of the country and some traits of the people which had escaped my attention; and thirdly, though I had seen much in America to arouse my admiration, I felt that, here and there, there was room for improvement, and to be compelled to criticize people who had been generous, courteous, and kind was something I did not wish to do. In answer to my scruples I was told that I was not expected to write about America in a partial or unfair manner, but to state impressions of the land just as I had found it. A lady friend, for whose opinion I have the highest respect, said in effect, "We want you to write about our country and to speak of our people in an impartial and candid way; we do not want you to bestow praise where it is undeserved; and when you find anything deserving of criticism or condemnation you should not hesitate to mention it, for we like our faults to be pointed out that we may reform." I admit the soundness of my friend's argument. It shows the broad-mindedness and magnanimity of the American people. In writing the following pages I have uniformly followed the principles laid down by my American lady friend. I have not scrupled to frankly and freely express my views, but I hope not in any carping spirit; and I trust American readers will forgive me if they find some opinions they cannot endorse. I assure them they were not formed hastily or unkindly. Indeed, I should not be a sincere friend were I to picture their country as a perfect paradise, or were I to gloss over what seem to me to be their defects.

Notes

* This magnificent building at The Hague, which is aptly called the Palace of Peace, was formally opened on the 28th of August, 1913, in the presence of Queen Wilhelmina, Mr. Carnegie (the founder) and a large assembly of foreign representatives.

** I refer to the Spanish-American War. Having captured the Philippine Islands, the United States paid $20,000,000, gold, for it to the Spanish Government.

*** This was several years ago. Fashions change every year. The present type is equally ludicrous.

1

The Importance of Names

'What's in a name? That which we call a rose
By any other name would smell as sweet.'

Notwithstanding these lines, I maintain that the selection of names is important. They should always be carefully chosen. They are apt to influence friendships or to excite prejudices according to their significance. We Chinese are very particular in this matter. When a son is born the father or the grandfather chooses a name for the infant boy which, according to his horoscope, is likely to insure him success, or a name is selected which indicates the wish of the family for the new-born child. Hence such names as "happiness", "prosperity", "longevity", "success", and others, with like propitious import, are common in China. With regard to girls their names are generally selected from flowers, fruits, or trees. Particular care is taken not to use a name which has a bad meaning. In Washington I once met a man in an elevator whose name was "Coffin". Was I to be blamed for wondering if the elevator would be my coffin? On another occasion I met a man whose name was "Death", and as soon as I heard his name I felt inclined to run away, for I did not wish to die. I am not superstitious. I have frequently taken dinner with thirteen persons at the table, and I do not hesitate to start on a journey on a Friday. I often do things which would not be done by superstitious persons in China. But to meet a man calling himself "Coffin" or "Death" was too much for me, and with all my disbelief in superstition I could not help showing some repugnance to those who bore such names.

Equally important, if not more so, is the selection of a name for a state or a nation. When the several states of America became independent they called themselves the "United States of America" - a very happy idea. The Union was originally composed of thirteen states, covering about 300,000 square miles; it is now composed of forty-eight states and three territories, which in area amount to 3,571,492 square miles, practically as large in extent as China, the oldest nation in the world. It should be noted that the name is most comprehensive: it might comprise the entire continent of North and South America. It is safe to say that the founders of the nation did not choose such a name without consideration, and doubtless the designation "United States of America" conceals a deep motive. I once asked a gentleman who said he was an American whether he had come from South or North America, or whether he was a Mexican, a Peruvian or a native of any of the countries in Central America? He replied with emphasis that he was an American citizen of the United States. I said it might be the United States of Mexico, or Argentina, or other United States, but he answered that when he called himself a citizen it could not mean any other than that of the United States of America. I have asked many other Americans similar questions and they all have given me replies in the same way. We Chinese call our nation "The Middle Kingdom"; it was supposed to be in the center of the earth. I give credit to the founders of the United States for a better knowledge of geography than that possessed by my countrymen of ancient times and do not assume that the newly formed nation was supposed to comprise the whole continent of North and South America, yet the name chosen is so comprehensive as to lead one naturally to suspect that it was intended to include the entire continent. However, from my observation of their national conduct, I believe their purpose was just and humane; it was to set a noble example to the sister nations in the Western Hemisphere, and to knit more closely all the nations on that continent through the bonds of mutual justice, goodwill and friendship. The American nation is, indeed, itself a pleasing and unique example of the principle of democracy. Its government is ideal, with a liberal constitution, which in effect declares that all men are created equal, and that the government is "of the people, for the people, and by the people." Anyone with ordinary intelligence and with open eyes, who should visit any city, town or village in America, could not but be impressed with the orderly and unostentatious way in which it is governed by the local authorities, or help being struck by the plain and democratic character of the people. Even in the elementary schools, democracy is taught and practised. I remember visiting a public school for children in Philadelphia, which I shall never forget. There were about three or four hundred children, boys and girls, between seven and fourteen years of age. They elected one of their students as mayor, another as judge, another as police commissioner, and in fact they elected for the control of their school community almost all the officials who usually govern a city. There were a few Chinese children among the students, and one of them was pointed out to me as the police superintendent. This not only eloquently spoke of his popularity, but showed goodwill and harmony among the several hundred children, and the entire absence of race feeling. The principals and teachers told me that they had no difficulty whatever with the students. If one of them did anything wrong, which was not often, he would be taken by the student policeman before the judge, who would try the case, and decide it on its merits, and punish or discharge his fellow student as justice demanded. I was assured by the school authorities that this system of self-government worked admirably; it not only relieved the teachers of the burden of constantly looking after the several hundred pupils, but each of them felt a moral responsibility to behave well, for the sake of preserving the peace and good name of the school. Thus early imbued with the idea of self-government, and entrusted with the responsibilities of its administration, these children, when grown up, take a deep interest in federal and municipal affairs, and, when elected for office, invariably perform their duties efficiently and with credit to themselves.

It cannot be disputed that the United States, with its democratic system of government, has exercised a great influence over the states and nations in

Central and South America. The following data showing the different nations of America, with the dates at which they turned their respective governments from monarchies into republics, all subsequent to the independence of the United States, are very significant.

Mexico became a republic in 1823, Honduras in 1839, Salvador in 1839, Nicaragua in 1821, Costa Rica in 1821, Panama in 1903, Colombia in 1819, Venezuela in 1830, Ecuador in 1810, Brazil in 1889, Peru in 1821, Bolivia in 1825, Paraguay in 1811, Chile in 1810, Argentina in 1824, and Uruguay in 1828.

These republics have been closely modelled upon the republican form of government of the United States; thus, nearly all the nations or states on the continent of America have become republics. Canada still belongs to Great Britain. The fair and generous policy pursued by the Imperial Government of Great Britain accounts for the Canadians' satisfaction with their political position, and for the fact that they do not wish a change. It must be noted, however, that a section of the American people would like to see Canada incorporated with the United States. I remember that at a public meeting held in Washington, at which Sir Wilfrid Laurier, then Premier of Canada, was present, an eminent judge of the Federal Supreme Court jocularly expressed a wish that Canada should be annexed to the United States. Later, Mr. Champ Clark, a leader of the Democratic Party in the House of Representatives, addressed the House urging the annexation of Canada. Even if these statements are not taken seriously they at least show the feelings of some people, and he would be a bold man who would prophesy the political status of Canada in the future. There is, however, no present indication of any change being desired by the Canadians, and it may be safely presumed that the existing conditions will continue for many years to come. This is not to be wondered at, for Canada, though nominally a British colony, practically enjoys almost all the privileges of an independent state. She possesses a constitution similar to that of the United Kingdom, with a parliament of two houses, called the "Senate", and the "House of Commons". The Sovereign of Great Britain appoints only the Governor General, who acts in his name, but the Dominion is governed by a responsible Ministry, and all domestic affairs are managed by local officials, without interference from the Home

Government. Canadians enjoy as many rights as the inhabitants of England, with the additional advantage that they do not have to bear the burden of maintaining an army and navy. Some years ago, if I remember rightly, in consequence of some agitation or discussion for independence, the late Lord Derby, then Secretary of State for the Colonies, stated that if the Canadians really wished for independence, the Home Government would not oppose, but that they should consider if they would gain anything by the change, seeing that they already had self-government, enjoyed all the benefits of a free people, and that the only right the Home Government reserved was the appointment of the Governor-General, although it assumed the responsibility of protecting every inch of their territory from encroachment. Since this sensible advice from the Colonial Secretary, I have heard nothing more of the agitation for independence.

From a commercial point of view, and for the welfare of the people, there is not much to choose today between a limited monarchy and a republic. Let us, for instance, compare England with the United States. The people of England are as free and independent as the people of the United States, and, though subjects, they enjoy as much freedom as Americans. There are, however, some advantages in favour of a republic. Americans until recently paid their President a salary of only $50,000 a year; it is now $75,000 with an additional allowance of $25,000 for travelling expenses. This is small indeed compared with the civil list of the King or Emperor of any great nation. There are more chances in a republic for ambitious men to distinguish themselves; for instance, a citizen can become a president, and practically assume the functions of a king or an emperor. In fact the President of the United States appoints his own cabinet officials, ambassadors, ministers, etc. It is generally stated that every new president has the privilege of making more than ten thousand appointments. With regard to the administration and executive functions he has in practice more power than is usually exercised by a king or an emperor of a constitutional monarchy. On the other hand, in some matters, the executive of a republic cannot do what a king or an emperor can do; for example, a president cannot declare war against a foreign nation without first obtaining the consent of Congress. In a monarchical government the king or the cabinet officials assume enormous

5

responsibilities. Lord Beaconsfield (then Mr. Disraeli), while he was Prime Minister of England, purchased in 1875 from the Khedive of Egypt 176,602 Suez Canal shares for the sum of 3,976,582 pounds on his own responsibility, and without consulting the Imperial Parliament. When Parliament or Congress has to be consulted about everything, great national opportunities to do some profitable business must undoubtedly be sometimes lost. No such bold national investment as that made by Lord Beaconsfield could have been undertaken by any American president on his own responsibility. Mr. Cleveland, when president of the United States, said that "the public affairs of the United States are transacted in a glass house."

Washington, in his farewell address, advised his compatriots that on account of the detached and distant situation of their country they should, in extending their commercial relations with foreign nations, have as little political connection with them as possible; and he asked this pertinent and pregnant question, "Why, by interweaving our destiny with that of any part of Europe, entangle our peace and prosperity in the toils of European ambition, rivalship, interest, humor, or caprice?" In 1823, twenty-seven years after Washington's celebrated address, President Monroe, in his annual message to Congress, warned the European Powers not to plant any new colonies on any portion of the American hemisphere, as any attempt on their part to extend their system in that part of the world would be considered as dangerous to the peace and safety of the United States. This "Monroe Doctrine," as it has since been called, practically protects every state and country on the American continent from attack or interference by any foreign power, and it cannot be denied that it has been and is now the chief factor in preserving the integrity of all the countries on that continent. Thus the United States is assuming the role of guardian over the other American nations. In the city of Washington there is an International Bureau of the American Republics, in which all the republics of Central and South America are represented. It is housed in a magnificent palace made possible by the beneficence of Mr. Andrew Carnegie, the American multi-millionaire and philanthropist, and the contributions of the different governments. It cost 750,000 gold dollars, and Mr. John Barrett, the capable and popular director of the Bureau, has well called it "a temple of friendship and commerce and a meeting place for the

American republics." The Bureau is supported by the joint contributions of the twenty-one American republics, and its affairs are controlled by a governing board composed of their diplomatic representatives in Washington, with the American Secretary of State as chairman *ex officio*. This institution no doubt strengthens the position of the United States and is calculated to draw the American republics into closer friendship.

2

American Prosperity

One of the main causes of the prosperity of the great American republic is its natural resources. It possesses coal, oil, silver, gold, copper, and all the other mineral ores. Nature seems, indeed, to have provided almost everything that man needs. The soil is rich; wheat and every kind of fruit can be grown; but favorable as are these native conditions they could not be turned to any great advantage without the skill and industry of enterprising men. Many countries in Africa and Asia possess equal advantages, but they are not equally prosperous. This leads me to the consideration of another reason for America's growth. The men who have migrated to the United States have not been rich people. They went there to make a living. They were prepared to work, their purpose was to improve their condition, and they were willing to undertake any manual or mental labor to accomplish their object. They were hardy and strong and could bear a heavy strain. Their children inherited their good qualities, and so an American is generally more hard-working and enterprising than most of the people in Europe and elsewhere.

Another reason for America's success is the great freedom which each citizen enjoys. Every man considers himself the equal of every other, and a young man who is ambitious will not rest until he reaches the top of his profession or trade. Thousands of Americans who were once very poor have become millionaires or multi-millionaires. Many of them had no college education, they taught themselves, and some of them have become both literary and scholarly. A college or university education does not necessarily make a man learned; it only gives him the opportunity to learn. It is said that some college men have proven themselves to be quite ignorant, or rather that they do not know so much as those who have been self-taught. I do not in any way wish to disparage a college education; no doubt men who have been trained in a university start in life with better prospects and with a greater chance of success, but those men who have not had such advantages have doubtless done much to make their country great and prosperous, and they ought to be recognized as great men.

The general desire of the American people to travel abroad is one of their good traits. People who never leave their homes cannot know much. A person may become well-informed by reading, but his practical knowledge cannot be compared with that of a person who has travelled. We Chinese are great sinners in this regard. A Chinese maxim says, "It is dangerous to ride on horseback or to go on a voyage;" hence until very recently we had a horror of going abroad. A person who remains all his life in his own town is generally narrow-minded, self-opinioned, and selfish. The American people are free from these faults. It is not only the rich and the well-to-do who visit foreign countries, but tradesmen and workmen, when they have saved a little money, also often cross the Atlantic. Some years ago a Senator in Washington told me that he crossed the Atlantic Ocean every summer and spent several months in Europe, and that the next trip would be his twenty-eighth voyage. I found, however, that he had never gone beyond Europe. I ventured to suggest that he should extend his next annual journey a little farther and visit Japan, China, and other places in the Far East which I felt sure he would find both interesting and instructive. I have travelled through many countries in Europe and South America, and wherever I have gone, and at whatever hotel I have put up, I have always found some Americans, and on many occasions I have met friends and acquaintances whom I had known in Washington or New York. But it is not only the men who go abroad; in many cases ladies also travel by themselves. On several occasions lady friends from Washington, Philadelphia, and New York have visited me in Peking. This is one of the Americans' strong points. Is it not wiser and much more useful to disburse a few hundred dollars or so in travelling and gaining knowledge, coming in to contact with other peoples and enlarging the mind, than to spend large sums of money on gaudy dresses, precious stones, trinkets, and other luxuries?

In a large country like America, where a considerable portion of the land still remains practically uncultivated or undeveloped, hardy, industrious, and patient workmen are a necessity. But the almost unchecked influx of immigrants who are not desirable citizens cannot but harm the country. In these days of international trade it is right that ingress and egress from one country to another should be unhampered, but persons who have committed crimes at home, or who are ignorant and illiterate, cannot become desirable citizens anywhere. They should be barred out of the United States of America. It is well known that foreigners take part in the municipal and federal affairs of the country as soon as they become citizens. Now if such persons really worked for the good of their adopted country, there could be no objection to this, but it is no secret that many have no such motives. That being so, it is a question whether steps should not be taken to limit their freedom. On the other hand, as many farms suffer from lack of workmen, people from whatever country who are industrious, patient, and persevering ought to be admitted as laborers. They would be a great boon to the nation. The fear of competition by cheap labor is causeless; regulations might be drawn up for the control of these foreign laborers, and on their arrival they could be drafted to those places where their services might be most urgently needed. So long as honest and steady workmen are excluded for no reason other than that they are Asiatics, while white men are indiscriminately admitted, I fear that the prosperity of the country cannot be considered permanent, for agriculture is the backbone of stable wealth. Yet at present it is the country's wealth which is one of the important factors of America's greatness. In the United States there are thousands of individuals whose fortunes are counted by seven or eight figures in gold dollars. And much of this money has been used to build railways, or to develop manufactories and other useful industries. The country has grown great through useful work, and not on account of the army and navy. In 1881 America's army numbered only 26,622 men, and her navy consisted of only 24 iron-clads, 2 torpedo-boats, and 25 tugs, but in 1910 the peace strength of her army was 96,628 and the navy boasted 33 battleships and 120 armoured cruisers of different sizes.

Within the last few years it has been the policy of many nations to increase the army and to build as many Dreadnaughts and Super-Dreadnaughts as possible. Many statesmen have been infected by this Dreadnaught fever. Their policy seems to be based on the idea that the safety of a nation depends on the number of its battleships. Even peaceful and moderate men are carried away by this hobby, and support it. It is forgotten that great changes have taken place during the last twenty or thirty years; that a nation can now be attacked by means quite beyond the reach of Dreadnaughts. The enormous sums spent on these frightful monsters, if applied to more worthy objects, would have a greater effect in preserving the nations' heritages than anything these monstrosities can do.

The nation which has a large army and a strong navy may be called powerful, but it cannot be considered great without other good requisites. I consider a nation as great when she is peacefully, justly, and humanely governed, and when she possesses a large number of benevolent and good men who have a voice in the administration. The greater the number of good men that a nation possesses the greater she becomes. America is known to have a large number of such men and women, men and women who devote their time and money to preaching peace among the nations. Mr. Andrew Carnegie is worth a hundred Dreadnaughts. He and others like him are the chief factors in safeguarding the interests and welfare of America. The territory of the United States is separated from Europe and other countries by vast oceans; so that it would be difficult, if not impossible, for a foe to successfully attack any portion of that country. But who wishes to attack her? She has scarcely an enemy. No country is invaded by another without cause, and as the United States is in friendly relations with all the Powers, there is no reason to fear foreign invasion. Even should a foreign power successfully attack her and usurp a portion of her territories, a supposition which is most improbable, would the enemy be able to hold what he seized? History shows that no conquered country has ever been successfully and permanently kept without the people's consent, and there is not the least chance that the Americans will ever consent to the rule of a foreign government.

It is to be hoped that the United States will not follow the example of other nations and unduly increase her armaments, but that she will take the lead in the universal peace movement and show the world that a great power can exist and maintain her position without force of arms. I am aware that general disarmament is not popular among statesmen, that it has been denounced by an eminent authority as a "will-o'-the wisp", that arbitration has been styled a "Jack-o'-lantern", but this is not the first time a good and workable scheme has been branded with opprobrious names. The abolition of slavery was at one time considered to be an insane man's dream; now all people believe in it. Will the twentieth century witness the collapse of our present civilization?

Why are the world's armaments constantly increasing? To my mind it is due to two causes, one of which is mistrust. One nation begins to build Dreadnaughts, another does the same through fear and mistrust. The second cause is that it is the fashion of some nations to follow the example of others that they may preserve their position as great naval powers. But it is unnecessary for the United States to show such mistrust or to follow such fashion. She should rather, as becomes a great and powerful nation, take an independent course of her own. If she sets the example other nations in due time will follow her. The peace of the world will be more surely guarded, and America will win the approbation, the respect, and the gratitude of all peace-loving people.

3

American Government

Democratic principles were enunciated by Chinese philosophers as long ago as 4,500 years, and from time to time various emperors and statesmen have endeavored to apply them to the government of China; but these principles, in all their minute details, have been exemplified only by the wisdom of the statesmen in the West. In the United States they are in full swing. As China has now become a republic, not in name only but in fact, it will be well for her statesmen and politicians to examine the American constitution, and to study its workings. To do this at close range it will be necessary for the student to visit Washington, the capital of the United States of America. Here he will find the President, or the chief of the nation. With the co-operation of his Cabinet and a large staff of assistants, the President administers the affairs of the Federal Government. He may be a new man and have had no previous training in diplomacy, and little administrative experience, but in all probability he is a man of resource and adaptability, who has mastered every detail of his high office. All important matters are referred to him, so that his daily work taxes his whole strength and energy. Another part of his function is to see the Congressmen, Senators, or Representatives, and others who call to see him on business, and this takes up a great part of his time. In fact, he is expected to be, and generally is, '*Suaviter in modo, fortiter in re.*'

In Washington, the National Congress, which is composed of the Senate and of the House of Representatives, holds its sittings in the Capitol, and passes bills subject to the approval of the President. If he signs a bill it becomes law, and binds the nation. The basic principle of democracy is the sovereignty of the people, but as the people cannot of themselves govern the country, they must delegate their power to agents who act for them. Thus they elect the Chief Magistrate to govern the country, and legislators to make the laws. The powers given to these agents are irrevocable during their respective terms of office. The electors are absolutely bound by their actions. Whatever laws Congress may pass, the people must strictly obey; thus the servants of the people really become their masters. There is no fear, however, that their masters *pro tempore* will betray their trust, as any neglect of duty on their part, or disregard of the wishes of their constituents, would most likely destroy their chances of re-election.

According to the terms of the Constitution, the senators and representatives must be residents of the states for which they are chosen. This is an excellent provision, insuring that the people's delegates possess local knowledge and know how to safeguard the interests and welfare of the states which sent them to Washington. On the other hand, as each state, irrespective of its size, is entitled to elect only two Senators, and to send only a limited number of Representatives to the House, proportionally to its population, unfortunately it frequently happens that eminent, capable, and well-known public men, of large experience, are deprived of an opportunity to serve their country. In England, and in some other lands, the electors may choose as their representative a resident of any city, borough, or county as they please, and it only occasionally happens that the member of Parliament actually lives in the district which he represents. Is it advisable to adopt a similar system in the United States? It could not be done without amending the Constitution, and this would not be easy; but every nation, as well as each individual, should be prepared, at all times, to receive fresh light, and be willing to change old customs to suit new conditions, and so I make the suggestion.

The fixing of four years as the term of office for the President was an excellent idea, intended no doubt to prevent an unpopular or bad President from remaining too long in power. It is, however, gradually dawning on the minds of intelligent people that this limited term, though excellent in theory, is very inconvenient in practice. However intelligent and capable a new President may be, several months must elapse before he can thoroughly understand all the details incidental to his exalted position, involving, in addition to unavoidable social functions, the daily reception of callers, and many other multifarious duties. By the time he has become familiar with these matters, and the work of the office is running smoothly, half of his term has gone; and should he aspire to a second term, which is quite natural, he must devote a great deal of time and attention to electioneering. Four years is plainly too short a period to give any President a chance to do justice either to himself or to the nation which entrusted him with his heavy responsibilities. Presidential elections are national necessities, but the less frequently they occur the better for the general welfare of the country. Those who have been in the United States during campaign years, and have seen the complicated working of the political machinery and all its serious consequences, will, I feel convinced, agree with what I say. During the greater part of the year in which a President has to be elected the entire nation is absorbed in the event, all the people, both high and low, being more or less keenly interested in the issue, and the preparations leading up to it. They seem to put everything else in the shade, and to give more attention to this than to anything else. Politicians and officials who have a personal interest in the result, will devote their whole time and energy to the work. Others who are less active, still, directly or indirectly, take their share in the electioneering. Campaign funds have to be raised and large sums of money are disbursed in many directions. All this sadly interrupts business; it not only takes many business men from their more legitimate duties, but it prevents merchants and large corporations from embarking in new enterprises, and so incidentally limits the demand for labor. In short, the whole nation is practically hurled into a state of bustle and excitement, and the general trade of the country is seriously affected. A young man in Washington, who was engaged to be married, once told me that he was too busy to think of marriage until the election was over.

If the French system were followed, and the President were elected by a majority of the combined votes of the Senate and the House of Representatives, the inconveniences, the excitements and expense above enumerated might be avoided, but I think the people of America would rather endure these evils than be deprived of the pleasure of electing their President themselves. The alternate remedy, so far as I can see, is to extend the presidential term to, say, six or seven years, without any chance of a re-election. If this proposal were adopted, the President would be more free and independent, he would not be haunted by the bugbear of losing his position by temporarily displeasing his political friends, he could give his undivided attention, as he cannot do now, to federal affairs, and work without bias or fear, and without interruption, for the welfare of his nation. He would have more chance of really doing something for his country which was worth while. A further advantage is that the country would not be so frequently troubled with the turmoil and excitement arising from the presidential election. If I were allowed to prophecy, I should say that the young republic of China, profiting by the experiences of France and America, will most likely adopt the French system of electing its President, or develop a system somewhat similar to it.

One of the defects in the American way of government is the spoils system, in accordance with the maxim, "To the victor belongs the spoils". The new President has the right of dismissing a large number of the holders of Federal Offices, and to appoint in their places his friends, or men of his party who have rendered it services, or who have otherwise been instrumental in getting him elected. I am told that thousands of officials are turned out in this way every four years. President Jackson introduced the practice, and almost every succeeding President has continued it. This spoils system has been adopted by almost every state and municipality; it forms indeed the corner-stone of practical politics in the United States. In every country, all over the world, there are cases where positions and places of emolument have been obtained through influential friends, but to dismiss public servants who are doing useful work, for no better reason than simply to make room for others, is very bad for the civil service, and for the country it serves. Attempts to remedy these evils have been made within recent years by the introduction of what is called "Civil Service Reform", by which a candidate is appointed to a post after an examination, and the term of his service is fixed. If this is to be strictly adhered to in all cases, the President will be, to a great extent, deprived of the means of rewarding his political friends. In that case I doubt if the professional politicians and wire pullers will be so active and arduous as they have hitherto been, as the chief aim in securing the election of the nominee will have been taken away. Great credit is due to President Taft for his courage and impartiality, in that after assuming the duties of the high office to which he was elected, he gave appointments to men according to their ability, irrespective of party claims, and even went so far as to invite one or two gentlemen of known ability who belonged to the opposite party to become members of his Cabinet.

In America men are not anxious for official offices. Men possessing talent and ability, with business acumen, are in great demand, and can distinguish themselves in their several professions in various ways; they can easily attain a position of wealth and influence, and so such men keep out of politics. It must not, however, be inferred from this that the government officials in America are incompetent. On the contrary I gladly testify from my personal experience that the work done by them is not only efficient, but that, taken as a whole, they compare most favorably with any other body of government officials in Europe. Still, on account of the small salaries paid, it is not to be wondered at that exceptionally good men cannot be induced to accept official positions. I have known several Cabinet Ministers who, after holding their offices for two or three years, were obliged to resign and resume their former business, and a President has been known to experience great difficulty in getting good and competent men to succeed them.

These remarks do not apply to the President, not because the President's salary is large, for compared with what European kings and emperors receive it is very small, but because the position is, far and above any other, the largest gift the people can bestow. No one has ever been known to refuse a presidential nomination. I believe anyone to whom it was offered would always gladly accept it. I have conversed with some in America who told me that they were heirs apparent to the White House, and so they are, for they are just as eligible candidates for the position, as is the Crown Prince to succeed to a throne in any European country. Even a lady was once nominated as a presidential candidate, although she did not obtain many votes.

One of the things which arouses my admiration is the due observance by the people of the existing laws and the Constitution. Every one obeys them, from the President to the peddler, without any exception. Sometimes, however, by a too strict and technical interpretation of the law, it works a hardship. Let me quote a case. According to Article 1, Section 6, of the Constitution, "no Senator or Representative shall, during the time for which he was elected, be appointed to any civil office under the authority of the United States, which shall have been created, or the emoluments whereof shall have been increased, during such time". A certain Senator was appointed by the President to a Cabinet office, but it happened that the salary attached to that office had been raised during the time he was in the Senate, and so it was held that he could draw only the salary which was allowed before he became a Senator, and that he was not entitled to the increase which was sanctioned by Congress while he was in the Senate, although at the time he had not the slightest notion that the increase would ever affect his own pocket.

The relation of the states to the Federal Government is peculiar and unique. I will illustrate my point by correcting a mistake often made by foreigners in regard to the different provinces of China. It is generally assumed by Western writers that each province in China is self-governed, and that the provincial authorities act independently and in defiance of the injunctions of the Peking Government. The facts, however, are that until the establishment of the Republic, all the officials in the Provinces were appointed or sanctioned by the Peking Government, and that by an Imperial decree even a Viceroy or Governor could, at any moment, be changed or dismissed, and that no important matter could be transacted without the Imperial sanction. How does this compare with the states in America? Every

American boasts that his state is independent of the Federal Government. All officials, from the Governor downward, are, in every state, elected by the people. Each state is provided with a legislature consisting of a Senate and a House of Representatives, also elected by the popular vote. The state has very large, and almost absolute, legislative and executive powers, and is competent to deal with all matters not reserved by the Constitution for the Federal Government. Each state is also independent of every other state. The criminal and civil laws, including all matters pertaining to the transfer of and the succession to property, as well as marriage, divorce and fiscal laws, are within the scope of the state administrations. The authorities of each state naturally do their best to make their own state as populous and prosperous as possible. Thus in some states the laws concerning divorce, corporations, and landed property are more favorable than in other states. A person, for example, unable to obtain a divorce in his own state, can, without difficulty, attain his object in another state. What is expressly prohibited by statute in one state may be perfectly legitimate in the neighboring state. It is the same with the local taxes; fees and taxes are not uniform; in one state they are heavy, while in another they are comparatively light. A stranger would naturally be surprised to find such a condition of things in a great nation like America, and would wonder how the machinery of such a government can work so well. Nevertheless he will find that everything goes on smoothly. This can be explained only by the fact that the inhabitants of one state often remove to other states, and by commercial and other dealings and social associations they mix together, so that, notwithstanding the dissimilarity of conditions in different states, the people easily adapt themselves to the local surroundings, and, so far as I can find, no friction or quarrel has ever arisen between two states. However, would it not be better for all the states to appoint an interstate committee to revise and codify their laws with a view to making them uniform?

Foreigners living in America sometimes find themselves at a disadvantage, owing to the state being independent of the control of the Federal Government. This point can be better illustrated by a case which happened some years ago in one of the states. A foreigner, who was the subject of a European country, was attacked by a mob, and his property destroyed. He laid his complaint before the local authorities, but it appeared that he could not obtain the redress he sought. His consul did all he could for him by appealing to the local authorities, but without success; finally the matter was reported to his ambassador in Washington, who immediately interested himself in the affair and brought it before the Secretary of State. The Secretary, after going into the facts of the case, said that all he could do was to write to the Governor of that state and request him to take the matter up, but the Governor, for some reason or other, did not take any such action as would have given satisfactory redress to the foreigner. His ambassador made frequent appeals to the Secretary of State, but the Secretary was powerless, as the Constitution does not empower the Federal Government to interfere in state matters. This seems a blemish in the administration of foreign affairs in the United States of America. Suppose a foreigner should be ill-treated or murdered in a state, and no proper redress be given, the Federal Government cannot send its officers to arrest the culprit. All it can do is to ask the Governor of that state to take action, and if he fail to do so there is no remedy. Fortunately such a case rarely happens, but for the more efficient carrying on of their state affairs, is it not better in special cases to invest the Federal Government with larger powers than those at present possessed by it? I am aware that this opens up a serious question; that Congress will be very reluctant to confer on the Federal Government any power to interfere in the state affairs, knowing that the states would not tolerate such an interference; but as there is a large and ever increasing number of aliens residing in the United States, it naturally follows that riots, and charges of ill treatment of foreigners now and then do occur. Now state officials can, as a rule, be trusted to deal with these matters fairly, but where local prejudice against a class of aliens runs high, is it not advisable to leave to the Federal officials, who are disinterested, the settlement of such cases? For the sake of cordial foreign relations, and to avoid international complications, this point, I venture to suggest, should be seriously considered by the Federal and the State Governments.

The question as to what form of government should be adopted by any country is not easy to decide. The people of America would no doubt claim that their system is the best, while the people of the monarchial governments in Europe would maintain that theirs is preferable. This is mostly a matter of education, and people who have been accustomed to their own form of government naturally like it best. There are communities who have been long accustomed to the old system of monarchial government, with their ancient traditions and usages. There are other communities, with a different political atmosphere, where all the people share in the public affairs of State. It would be manifestly improper to introduce a democratic government among the former. It would not suit their tastes nor fit in with their ideas. What is good for one nation is not necessarily good for another. Each system of government has its good points, provided that they are faithfully and justly carried out. The aim to secure the happiness and comfort of the people and to promote the peace and prosperity of the nation should always be kept in view. As long as these objects can be secured it does not matter much whether the government is monarchial, republican, or something else.

It may pertinently be asked why China has become a republic, since from time immemorial she has had a monarchial form of government. The answer is that the conditions and circumstances in China are peculiar, and are different from those prevailing in Japan and other countries. In Japan it is claimed that the Empire was founded by the first Emperor, Jummu Tenno, 660 B.C. and that the dynasty founded by him has continued ever since. It is well known that the Chinese Imperial family is of Manchu origin. The Ching dynasty was founded in 1644 by conquest, not by succession. Upon the recent overthrow of the Manchu dynasty it was found very difficult to find a Chinese, however popular and able, who possessed the legal right of succeeding to the throne. Jealousy and provincial feelings placed this suggestion absolutely beyond discussion. Disagreements, frictions, and constant civil war would have ensued if any attempt had been made to establish a Chinese dynasty. Another fact is that a large majority of the intelligent people of China were disgusted with the system of monarchial government. Thus it will be seen that for the sake of the peace and welfare of the nation there was no other course for the people but to take a long jump and to establish the present republic. The law of evolution has been very actively at work in China, and no doubt it will be for her ultimate good, and therefore for the benefit of all mankind. China is now an infant republic, but she will grow into a healthy and strong youth. Her people have the kindest feeling for the people of the elder republic across the Pacific. There are excellent reasons why the two republics should be in closer friendship. It is well known that there are great potentialities for the expansion of trade in China, and as the Philippine Islands are close to our shores, and the completion of the Panama Canal will open a new avenue for the enlargement of trade from America, it will be to the interest of both nations to stretch out their hands across the Pacific in the clasp of good fellowship and brotherhood. When this is done, not only will international commerce greatly increase, but peace, at least in the Eastern Hemisphere, will be better secured than by a fleet of Dreadnaughts.

4

America and China

America has performed great service for the Orient and especially for China. If, however, the people of the latter country were asked to express their candid opinion on the matter, the verdict would not be altogether pleasant, but would be given with mixed feelings of gratitude and regret. Since the formal opening of China to foreign trade and commerce, people of all nationalities have come here, some to trade, some for pleasure, some to preach Christianity, and others for other purposes. Considering that the Chinese have a civilization of their own, and that their modes of thoughts, ideas, and habits are, in many respects, different from those of the Western people, it is not surprising that frictions and disputes have occasionally occurred and that even foreign wars have been waged between China and the Occident, but it is gratifying to observe that no force has ever been resorted to against China by the United States of America. Now and then troublesome questions have arisen, but they have always been settled amicably. Indeed the just and friendly attitude taken by the American officials in China had so won the esteem and confidence of the Chinese Government that in 1867, on the termination of Mr. Anson Burlingame's term as American Minister to Peking, he was appointed by the Manchu Government as Chief of a special mission to America and Europe. In that capacity he performed valuable services for China, although his work was unfortunately cut short by his untimely death. The liberal and generous treatment accorded to Chinese students in America is another source of satisfaction. They have been admitted freely to all educational institutions, and welcomed into American families. In whatever school or college they enter they are taught in the same way as the American boys and girls, and enjoy equal opportunities of learning all that the American students learn.* That America has no desire for territorial acquisition in China is well known. During the Boxer movement the American Government took the lead in initiating the policy of maintaining an open door, and preserving the integrity of China, a policy to which the other great powers readily consented. It was well known at the time, and it is no breach of confidence to mention the fact here, that Mr. John Hay, American Secretary of State, with the permission of President McKinley, was quite willing that America's indemnity demanded from China as her share of the compensation for losses sustained during the Boxer upheaval should be reduced by one-half, provided the other powers would consent to similar reductions. Unfortunately, Mr. Hay's proposal could not be carried out for want of unanimity. However, to show the good faith, and the humane and just policy of America, she has since voluntarily refunded to China a considerable portion of her indemnity, being the surplus due to her after payment of the actual expenses incurred. This is the second occasion on which she has done this, although in the previous case the refund was smaller. These are some of the instances for which the people of China have good reasons to be grateful to America and her people.

There is, however, another side to the picture; the Chinese students in America, who may be roughly calculated by the thousands, and whose number is annually increasing, have been taught democratic principles of government. These could not but be detrimental to the welfare of the late Manchu Government. They have read the history of how the American people gained their independence, and naturally they have been imbued with the idea of inaugurating a similar policy in China. Chinese merchants, traders, and others who have been residing in America, seeing the free and independent manner in which the American people carry on their government, learned, of course, a similar lesson. These people have been an important factor in the recent overthrow of the Manchu dynasty. Added to this, the fact that America has afforded a safe refuge for political offenders was another cause of dissatisfaction to the Manchus. Thus it will be seen that the Manchu Government, from their point of view, have had many reasons for entertaining unfavorable sentiments toward America.

This view, I need hardly say, is not shared by the large majority of Chinese. Persons who have committed political offenses in their own country find protection not only in America but in all countries in Europe, Japan, and other civilized lands. It is an irony of fate that since the establishment of the Chinese republic, Manchu and other officials under the old regime now find secure asylums in Hongkong, Japan, and Tsingtao, while hundreds of ex-Manchu officials have fled to the foreign settlements of Shanghai, Tientsin, and other treaty ports so reluctantly granted by the late Manchu Government. Thus the edge of their complaint against America's policy in harboring political refugees has been turned against themselves, and the liberality against which they protested has become their protection.

The more substantial cause for dissatisfaction with the United States is, I grieve to say, her Chinese exclusion policy. As long as her discriminating laws against the Chinese remain in force a blot must remain on her otherwise good name, and her relations with China, though cordial, cannot be perfect. It is beyond the scope of this chapter to deal with this subject exhaustively, but in order to enable my readers to understand the exact situation it is necessary to supply a short historical summary. In 1868, on account of the pressing need of good laborers for the construction of railways and other public works in America, the Governments of China and the United States concluded a treaty which provided that "Chinese subjects visiting or residing in the United States shall enjoy the same privileges, immunities, and exemptions in respect to travel or residence as may be enjoyed by the citizens or subjects of the most favored nation." It was a treaty negotiated by that great

American statesman, Secretary Seward, and announced by the President of the United States to Congress as a "liberal and auspicious treaty." It was welcomed by the United States as a great advance in their international relations. It had also the double significance of having been negotiated by a Chinese special embassy, of which a distinguished American diplomat, Mr. Anson Burlingame, who was familiar with the wishes and interests of the American people, was the head.

But within a few years the labor unions on the Pacific coast began to object to the competition of Chinese laborers. Soon afterward, the Chinese Government, to its intense surprise, was informed that the President of the United States had delegated a commission to come to Peking to solicit an abrogation of the treaty clause to which reference has been made. The Chinese Government was naturally unwilling to abrogate a treaty which had been urged on her by the United States with so much zeal, and which had so lately been entered upon on both sides with such high hopes. Long and tedious negotiations ensued, and finally a short treaty was concluded, the first and second Articles of which are as follows:

Article I

Whenever in the opinion of the Government of the United States, the coming of Chinese laborers to the United States, or their residence therein, affects or threatens to affect the interests of that country, or to endanger the good order of the said country or of any locality within the territory thereof, the Government of China agrees that the Government of the United States may regulate, limit, or suspend such coming or residence, but may not absolutely prohibit it. The limitation or suspension shall be reasonable and shall apply only to Chinese who may go to the United States as laborers, other classes not being included in the limitations. Legislation taken in regard to Chinese laborers will be of such a character only as is necessary to enforce the regulation, limitation, or suspension of immigration, and immigrants shall not be subject to personal maltreatment or abuse.

Article II

> Chinese subjects, whether proceeding to the United States as teachers, students, merchants, or from curiosity, together with their body and household servants, and Chinese laborers who are now in the United States shall be allowed to go and come of their own free will and accord, and shall be accorded all the rights, privileges, immunities, and exceptions which are accorded to the citizens and subjects of the most favored nations.

It would seem reasonable to expect that in yielding so fully to the wishes of the United States in this second negotiation the Chinese Government would not be called upon to make any further concessions in the interests or at the demand of the labor unions on the Pacific coast, but in this China was disappointed. Within a period of less than ten years an urgent application was made by the American Secretary of State for a new treaty amended so as to enable the Congress of the United States to still further restrict the privileges of Chinese laborers who had come to the United States. And when the Chinese Government hesitated to consent to the withdrawal of rights which the United States granted to the subjects of other Governments, Congress passed the Scott Act of 1888, prohibiting any Chinese person from entering the United States except Chinese officials, teachers, students, merchants or travellers for pleasure or curiosity, and forbidding also Chinese laborers in the United States, after having left, from returning thereto. This, in the words of Hon. J. W. Foster, ex-Secretary of State and a distinguished international lawyer, "was a deliberate violation of the Treaty of 1880 and was so declared by the Supreme Court of the United States." In order to save the Executive of the United States from embarrassment, the Chinese Government, contrary to its own sense of justice and of international comity, for a third time yielded to the wishes of the United States, and concluded the amended treaty of 1894, which gave Congress additional power of legislation respecting Chinese laborers. By Article I of this treaty it was agreed that for a term of ten years the coming of Chinese laborers to the United States should be absolutely prohibited. Article II distinctly provided that "the provisions of this convention shall not affect the right at present enjoyed of Chinese subjects, being officials, teachers, students, merchants, or travellers for curiosity or pleasure, but not laborers, of coming to the United States and residing therein." Thus it is clear that the prohibition affects only laborers, and not the other classes of Chinese. For a few years after the signing of this convention this was the view adopted and acted upon by the immigration officials, but afterward they changed their attitude, and the foregoing Article has since been interpreted to mean that only the above-mentioned five classes can be admitted into the United States, and that all the other classes of Chinese, however respectable and honorable, must be refused admission. Will my readers believe that a Chinese banker, physician, lawyer, broker, commercial agent, scholar or professor could all be barred out of the United States of America under the provisions of this convention? In the face of the plain language of the text it seems too absurd and unreasonable to be contemplated, and yet it is a fact.

This convention was proclaimed in December, 1894. According to its provisions, it was to remain in force only for a period of ten years, but that if six months before the end of that period neither power should give notice of denunciation, it should be extended for a similar period. Such notice was, however, given by China to the United States and accordingly the convention expired in December, 1904, and is now no longer in force. No serious attempt has since been made by the United States Government to negotiate a new treaty regarding Chinese laborers, so the customs and immigration officials continue to prohibit Chinese laborers from coming to America by virtue of the law passed by Congress. It will be seen that by the treaty of 1868, known as the "Burlingame Treaty," the United States Government formally agreed that Chinese subjects, visiting or residing in the United States, should enjoy the same privileges and immunities as were enjoyed by the citizens or subjects of the most favored nation; that being so, and as the convention of 1894 has expired, according to the legal opinion of Mr. John W. Foster, and other eminent lawyers, the continuation of the exclusion of Chinese laborers and the restrictions placed upon Chinese merchants and others seeking admission to the United States are not only without international authority but in violation of treaty stipulations.

The enforcement of the exclusion laws against the Chinese in the Hawaiian and Philippine Islands is still more inexcusable. The complaint in America against the immigration of Chinese laborers was that such immigration was detrimental to white labor, but in those islands there has been no such complaint; on the contrary the enforcement of the law against the Chinese in Hawaii has been, and is, contrary to the unanimous wish of the local Government and the people. Free intercourse and immigration between those islands and China have been maintained for centuries. What is most objectionable and unfair is that the Chinese should be singled out for discrimination, while all other Asiatics such as Japanese, Siamese, and Malays are allowed to enter America and her colonies without restraint. It is my belief that the gross injustice that has been inflicted upon the Chinese people by the harsh working of the exclusion law is not known to the large majority of the American people, for I am sure they would not allow the continuation of such hardships to be suffered by those who are their sincere friends. China does not wish special treatment, she only asks that her people shall be treated in the same way as the citizens or subjects of other countries. Will the great American nation still refuse to consent to this?

To solve the problem of immigration in a manner that would be satisfactory to all parties is not an easy task, as so many conflicting interests are involved. But it is not impossible. If persons interested in this question be really desirous of seeing it settled, and are willing to listen to reasonable proposals, I believe that a way may be found for its solution. There is good reason for my optimistic opinion. Even the Labor Unions, unless I am mistaken, would welcome an amicable settlement of this complicated question. In 1902, while at Washington, I was agreeably surprised to receive a deputation of the leaders of the Central Labor Union of Binghamton, New York, inviting me to pay a visit there and to deliver an address. As I did not wish to disappoint them I accepted their invitation. During my short stay there, I was very cordially and warmly received, and most kindly treated not only by the local authorities and inhabitants, but by the members of the Labor Union and the working men also. I found that the Union leaders and the working men were most reasonable, their platform being, as far as I could learn, to have no cheap labor competition, but not necessarily discrimination against any race. If the United States Government would appoint a commission composed of members representing the Labor Unions, manufacturers and merchants, to treat with a similar commission nominated by the Chinese Government, the whole question in all its bearings could be discussed, and I feel certain that after free and candid exchange of views, the joint Commissioners would be able to arrive at a scheme which would put at rest once and for all the conflicting claims, and settle the matter satisfactorily to both China and the United States.

When this disagreeable difference has been removed, the friendly relations between the two republics, cordial even while one was yet an Empire, will leave nothing to be desired and cannot but help to largely affect the trade between the two countries and to contribute to the peace of the Far East.

Notes

* I need hardly say that our students are also well treated in England, France, Germany, Japan, and other countries in Europe, but I am dealing in this chapter with America.

5

American Education

Out of a total population of 91,972,266 in the United States there were, in 1910, 17,506,175 pupils enrolled. Few nations can show such a high percentage of school students. The total number of teachers was 506,040. Educational efficiency on such a scale can be maintained only by a large expenditure of money, and from the statistics of education I find that the sum received from tuition fees was $14,687,192 gold, from productive funds $11,592,113 gold, and from the United States Government $4,607,298 gold, making a total of $70,667,865 gold. I question whether any other nation can produce such an excellent example in the cause of education.

In every state there are very many schools, both public and private. There are public schools in every town, and even the smallest village has its school, while in some agricultural states, such as Wyoming, where the population is very scattered, teachers are provided by the government to teach in the farmers' homes wherever three or four children can be gathered together. The public schools are free and open to all, but in some towns in the Southern States special schools are provided for the colored people. Having such facilities for gaining knowledge, it naturally follows that the Americans, as a whole, are an educated people. By this I mean the native American, not the recent immigrants and negroes, but even as regards the latter a reservation should be made, for some of the negroes, such as Booker T. Washington and others, have become eminent through their learning and educational work.

The distinguishing feature of the school system is that it is cheap and comprehensive. In the primary and high schools the boys and girls, whether they come from the wealthy or aristocratic families, or from more straitened homes, are all studying together in the same classroom, and it is known that a President sent his son to study in a public school. There is, therefore, no excuse for even the poorest man in America being an illiterate. If he wishes he can obtain a degree in a university without difficulty. Many of the state universities admit the children of citizens of the state free, while their tuition fees for outsiders are exceptionally low, so that it is within the power of a man of the most moderate means to give his son a university education. Many of the college or university students, in order to enable them to go through their courses of study, do outside jobs after their lecture hours, and perform manual, or even menial work, during the vacations. I frequently met such students in summer resorts acting as hotel waiters and found them clean, attentive, and reliable. During a visit to Harvard University, President Eliot took me to see the dining-hall. Many students were taking their lunch at the time. I noticed that the waiters were an unusually clean set of young men, and upon inquiry was informed that they were students of the University, and that when a waiter was wanted many students applied, as the poorer students were glad to avail themselves of the opportunity to earn some money.

Honest labor, though menial, is not considered degrading, and no American of education and refinement is above doing it. In some of the states in the East, owing to the scarcity of servants, families do their own cooking and other household work. Some few years ago I was on a visit to Ashburnham, Massachusetts, and was surprised to find that my hostess not only did the cooking but also cleaned my room. I was invited to a formal luncheon by a professor, and to my astonishment his two daughters waited at the table. This is not unlike what occurs in some parts of China in the interior. The members of families, although in good circumstances, do their own household work. In some towns, not far from Canton, wealthy farmers and country gentlemen hire out their sons as menials, so that these youngsters, when they have grown up, shall know the value of money and not squander the family wealth. I cite a typical case of a millionaire who had only one son. In order to make him appreciate the worth of money he took his boy to Canton, and allowed him to be hired out as an ordinary servant. The boy was ordered by his master to look after a certain part of the house, and also to take care of a little garden. One day he carelessly broke a valuable goldfish jar much prized by the family. His master naturally became enraged and reproached him for his negligence. The young man coolly told him that if he would come to his father's house he could replace the broken vessel by making his own selection from his father's collection of goldfish jars. This irritated the master, who thought that the lad was adding insult to injury. However, ultimately, his master was persuaded to go with him to his father's house, and to his great astonishment he found there many goldfish jars which were more precious than that which the lad had broken. Household work, however mean it may be, is not considered degrading in China, but the difference between China and America is that in America the people are compelled to do it from necessity, while in China it is resorted to as a matter of policy to make the young men realize the value of money, and not spend it wastefully.

The curriculum prescribed in schools covers a wide range of subjects, and the graduates are well equipped to face the battle of life. Not only are drawing, sketching and other fine arts taught, but also carpentry and other trades. I was once shown a fairly made box which was the product of a very small boy. I did not at first perceive the use of teaching a boy to do such work in school, but I learned that its object was to instruct the pupil how to think and arrange his materials systematically.

With the exception of those schools established by Christian societies, or endowed by religious sects, all educational institutions, especially those established by the state authorities, are secular. Religion is not taught. Neither the Bible nor any other religious work is used in the schoolroom. The presidents, professors, and tutors may be strict churchmen, or very religious people, but, as a rule, they are not permitted to inculcate their religious views on the students. The minds of the young are most susceptible, and if no moral principles are impressed upon them at school or college they are apt to go astray. It should be remembered that men of education without moral principles are like a ship without an anchor. Ignorant and illiterate people infringe the law because they do not know any better, and their acts of depredation are clumsy and can be easily found out, but when men of education commit crimes these are so skilfully planned and executed that it is difficult for the police to unravel and detect them. It has been known that frauds and forgeries perpetrated by such unscrupulous persons were so cleverly designed that they bore the evidence of superior education, and almost of genius. The more a man is educated the more is it necessary, for the welfare of the state, to instruct him how to make a proper use of his talents: education is like a double-edged sword. It may be turned to dangerous usages if it is not properly handled.

As there is no established church in the United States, and in view of the numberless different sects, it is not advisable to permit any particular phase of religion to be taught. But why not consent to allow the cardinal principles of morality to be taught in every school? The following may serve as examples:

1. Honesty is the best policy.
2. Honor thy father and thy mother.
3. Universal brotherhood.
4. Love of mankind.
5. Charity to all.
6. Purity in thought and action.
7. Pure food makes a pure body.
8. Happiness consists of health and a pure conscience.
9. Live and let live.
10. Respect a man for his virtues, not for his money or position.
11. 'Fiat justitia, ruat coelum' (Let justice be done, though the Heavens should fall).
12. Bear no malice against anyone.

13. Be equitable and just to all men.
14. Liberty and freedom but not license.
15. Do not unto others what ye would not that others should do unto you.

I have jotted down the above just as they occurred to me while writing. They can easily be amplified, and be made the basis of an ethical instruction in all the schools. In any case, every nation should aim at the highest standard of morals.

Co-education in the United States is not so unpopular as in some other countries, and it is increasing in favor. In all the primary schools, and in most of the high schools, boys and girls study in the same classroom, and girls are admitted as students even in some colleges and universities. This principle of admitting the fair sex to equal educational privileges is slowly but surely being recognized everywhere. In some universities the authorities have gone half-way; lectures are given to the girl students in separate rooms; or separate buildings, or halls, are provided for the girl students. With regard to the teaching staff, in the primary schools nearly all the teachers are women, and in the high schools their number is at least half, if not more. In some of the universities there are lady professors or tutors. It goes without saying that girls have the natural talent for learning everything that boys can learn. The objections raised by the opponents of co-education seem to rest chiefly upon the danger of the intellectual or physical overstrain of girls during adolescence, and upon the unequal rate of development of boys and girls during the secondary school period. It is further alleged that in mixed schools the curriculum is so prescribed that the girls' course of study is more or less adapted to that of the boys, with the result that it cannot have the artistic and domestic character which is suitable for the majority of girls; but why should not the curriculum be arranged in such a way as to suit both sexes? Is it not good for both to learn the same subjects? That which is good for a boy to learn, is it not equally advisable for a girl to know, and vice versa? Will not such a policy create mutual sympathy between the sexes? The opponents of the co-education policy assert that it makes the girls masculine, and that it has a tendency to make the boys a little feminine. It cannot, however, be doubted that the system reduces the cost of education, such as the duplication of the teaching staff, laboratories, libraries, and other equipment.

It is objected that the system has done more than anything else to rob marriage of its attractions by divesting man of most of his old-time glamour and romance. It is claimed that this early contact with the other sex, on a footing of equality, and the manner in which the majority of the girl students more than maintain their intellectual standing with the boys, has tended to produce that contempt of the much-vaunted superiority of man, that, as a rule, is reserved for those post-nuptial discoveries which make marriage such an interesting venture. But they forget that marriages are frequently contracted in places where girls and boys are taught together, and where they have had ample opportunities for knowing each other intimately, and that experience proves that such marriages are happy and lasting unions. It is interesting to observe, however, that as the number of educational institutions has increased, the number of unmarried women has been correspondingly augmented. It is easy to explain this by the fact that a large number of women earn their own livelihood by going into business and the professions. As they become more educated, and are allowed to participate in many of the same privileges as men, it is only natural that they should show their independence by remaining single. The same thing would occur in any country, and we may expect a like state of things in China as greater facilities for instruction are afforded to women. I do not feel alarmed at the prospect; indeed, I would welcome it if I could see my countrywomen acting as independently and as orderly as their American sisters.

The games and sports sanctioned and encouraged in schools and universities are useful, in that they afford diversion of the pupils' minds from their school work. They should not, however, be indulged in in such a way as to interfere with their studies. Take, as an example, boat racing; several months of preparation are necessary before the event takes place, and during a great portion of this time the students do not think much of their studies; they are all mad with excitement. The contest between the two rival parties is very keen; they have but one thought, and that is to win the race. In this way, at least so it seems to me, the main object of recreation is entirely lost sight of; it becomes no longer an amusement, but labor and work. I am told that the coxswain and the other members of the boat race generally have to take a long rest when the race is over, which clearly shows that they have been overworking. I favor all innocent games and sports which mean recreation and diversion, but if it be thought that without a contest games would lose their relish and their fun, then I would suggest that the aim should be the exhibition of a perfect body and absolute health. Let the students, when they come to the recreation ground, indulge in any sport they please, but make them feel that it is "bad form" to overstrain, or do anything which, even temporarily, mars the perfect working of their physical organisms. Let each student so train himself as to become healthy and strong both physically and mentally, and the one who, through reasonable and wholesome exercises, is able to present himself in the most perfect health should be awarded the highest prize.

6

American Business Methods

If I should be asked what is most essential for the successful carrying on of business in America, I would say advertising. A business man in America who intends to succeed must advertise in the daily, weekly, and monthly papers, and also have big posters in the streets. I do not believe any up-to-date merchant in America fails to do this. Every book and magazine contains many advertisements; sometimes fully half of a big magazine is covered with notices or pictures of articles for sale. Wherever you go the inevitable poster confronts you; and even when you look out of the window of the train you see large sign-boards announcing some article of trade. The newer the brand the bigger the picture. If, when you get into a streetcar, you look around you will see nothing but advertisements of all kinds and sorts, and if you answer an advertisement you will keep on receiving notices of the matter about which you inquired. Even now I receive letters urging me to buy something or other about which I sent a letter of inquiry when I was in America. At night, if you stroll round the town you will be amazed by the ingenious and clever signs which the alert minds of the tradespeople have invented, such as revolving electric lights forming the name of the advertiser with different colors, or a figure or shape of some sort illustrating his wares. But even this is not thought sufficient. Circulars are often sent to everyone, making special offers, setting forth forceful reasons why the commodity advertised is indispensable. Certain stores make it a point to announce cheap sales once or twice a year, with from 10 to 25 percent reduction. It should be noted that no tradesman voluntarily sells his goods at a loss, so that if during a sale he can give as much as 25 percent discount we can easily calculate the percentage of profit he generally makes. There are cases where men who started as petty dealers have, after a few years, become millionaires.

To show the importance of advertising I cite a well-known sanitary drink which is a substitute for tea and coffee, and which, by extensive advertising in almost every paper published in every country, has now become a favorite beverage. The proprietor is now a multi-millionaire and I am told that he spends more than a million dollars a year in advertising.

Another thing inseparable from American business is the telephone. A telephone is a part of every well-appointed house, every partner's desk is provided with a telephone, through which he talks to his clients and transacts business with them. In all official departments in Washington scores of telephones are provided; even the secretary of the department and the chief of the bureau give orders by telephone. It goes without saying that this means of communication is also found in the home of almost every well-to-do family. The invention of the telephone is a great blessing to mankind; it enables friends to talk to each other at a distance without the trouble of calling. Sweethearts can exchange their sweet nothings, and even proposals of marriage have been made and accepted through the telephone. However, one is subjected to frequent annoyances from wrong connections at the Central Office, and sometimes grave errors are made. Once, through a serious blunder, or a mischievous joke, I lost a dinner in my Legation in Washington. My valet received a telephone message from a lady friend inviting me to dine at her house. I gladly accepted the invitation, and at the appointed time drove to her home, only to find that there was no dinner-party on, and that I should have to go hungry.

With some trades, in order to create a new market, commercial travellers, or "drummers," give their goods away for nothing. Experience has proved that what they lose at the start they recover in the course of time, receiving in addition triple or tenfold more business than the cost of the original outlay. These commercial agents travel through all sections of the country to solicit business; they call upon those who can give them orders; they look up those who are engaged in similar businesses to their own, and, if they are retailers, they invite their orders, or ask them to become sub-agents. These gentlemen practically live on the trains: they eat, sleep, and do their business while travelling. One of them told me that in one month he had covered 38,000 miles, and that he had not been back to his firm for three months.

There is no doubt that the American people are active, strenuous workers. They will willingly go any distance, and undertake any journey, however arduous, if it promises business; they seem to be always on the go, and they are prepared to start anywhere at a moment's notice. An American who called on me a short time ago in Shanghai told me that when he left his house one morning at New York, he had not the slightest notion he was going to undertake a long journey that day; but that when he got to his office his boss asked him if he would go to China on a certain commission. He accepted the responsibility at once and telephoned to his wife to pack up his things. Two hours later he was on a train bound for San Francisco where he boarded a steamer for China. The same gentleman told me that this trip was his second visit to China within a few months.

American salesmen are clever and capable, and well know how to recommend whatever they have to sell. You walk into a store just to look around; there may be nothing that you want, but the adroit manner in which the salesman talks, and the way in which he explains the good points of every article at which you look, makes it extremely difficult for you to leave the store without making some purchases. Salesmen and commercial travellers in the United States have certainly learned the art of speaking. I once, however, met a remarkable exception to this rule in the person of an American gentleman who was singularly lacking in tact; he was in China with the intention of obtaining a concession, and he had nearly accomplished his object when he spoilt everything by his blunt speech. He said he had not come to China for any philanthropic purposes, but that he was in the country to make money. We all know that the average business man is neither a Peabody nor a Carnegie, but it was quite unnecessary for this gentleman to announce that his sole object was to make money out of the Chinese.

Up to a few years ago business men in America, especially capitalists, had scarcely any idea of transacting business in China. I well remember the difficulty I had in raising a railway loan in America. It was in 1897. I had received positive instructions from my government to obtain a big loan for the purpose of constructing the proposed railway from Hankow to Canton. I endeavored to interest well-known bankers and capitalists in New York City but none of them would consider the proposals. They invariably said that their money could be just as easily, and just as profitably, invested in their own country, and with better security, than was obtainable in China. It was only after nearly twelve months of hard work, of careful explanation and much persuasion, that I succeeded in finding a capitalist who was prepared to discuss the matter and make the loan. Conditions have now changed. American bankers and others have found that investments in China are quite safe. They have sent agents to China to represent them in the matter of a big international loan, and they are now just as ready to lend money in China as in Europe, and on the same terms. In conjunction with the representatives of some large European capitalists they even formed a powerful syndicate in China, for the purpose of arranging loans to responsible Chinese investors. In the spring of 1913, however, they withdrew from the syndicate.

The opportunities to make money in America are great and a young man with only fair ability, but an honest purpose, will always get something to do; and if he is industrious and ready for hard work, if he possess courage and perseverance, he will most surely go forward and probably in time become independent. There are hundreds of millionaires and multi-millionaires in America who, in their younger days, were as poor as sparrows in a snowstorm, but through perseverance, combined with industrious and economical habits, they have prospered far beyond their own expectations. The clever methods they adopt in the carrying on of their business cannot but arouse our admiration, and Chinese merchants would do well to send some of their sons to America to study the various systems practised there. But no nation or any class of people is perfect, and there is one money-making device which seems to me not quite sound in principle. To increase the capital of a corporation new shares are sometimes issued, without a corresponding increase in the actual capital. These new shares may represent half, or as much of the actual capital as has been already subscribed. Such a course is usually defended by the claim, that as the property and franchises have increased in value since the formation of the corporation, the increase of the stock is necessary in order to fairly represent the existing capital. It is said that some railway stock has been "watered" in this way to an alarming extent, so that a great deal of it is fictitious, yet though it exists only on paper it ranks as the equal of the genuine stock when the dividends are paid. Whether or not such an action really is justifiable, or even moral, I leave to the Christian clergy and their followers to decide. The promoters and directors of such concerns have at least hit upon a very clever method for becoming rich, and if the securities of the original shareholders are not injured, and the holders of the genuine and the watered stock can share equally without endangering the interests of all, perhaps such an action may be less blamable, but it is a new kind of proceeding to Orientals.

I must not omit to mention, however, the confidence which is placed in the honesty of the people in general; for example, when you enter an omnibus, you will find the driver, but no conductor to collect the fare. It is "up to you" to put the fare into a box, and if you do not pay no one will ask for it. Yet every fare is paid. I have never seen a dishonest man who omitted to pay. This is a remarkable fact which I have noticed nowhere but in America. I suppose it is because the people are not poor, and as they are always able to pay the fare they do so. They are too honest to cheat. It is certainly a good way to encourage people to be honest, to put them on their honor and then rely on their own sense of uprightness.

The most curious sight I have ever seen was the Stock Exchange in New York. It is used as a market for the purchase and sale of various articles, but there were no goods exposed for sale. I saw a good many people running about talking, yelling and howling, and had I not been informed beforehand what to expect I should have thought that the men were getting ready, in their excitement, for a general all-round fight. However, I did not see any exchange of blows, and I did not hear that any blood was shed.

Another remarkable feature of the scene was that I did not see a single woman there; she was conspicuous by her absence. Whether or not the rules of the Exchange allow her to become a member I do not know, that is a question for the woman suffragists to investigate; but I learned that it is a wealthy association consisting of 1,100 members, and that to become a member one must be a citizen of the United States of 21 years of age or more. The number of members is limited. Persons obtain membership by election, or by the transfer of the membership of a member who has resigned or died. A new member who is admitted by transfer pays an initiation fee of 2,000 gold dollars, in addition to a large fee to the transferrer, for his "seat in the House". A member may transfer his seat to his son, if the Committee of the Exchange approve, without charging for it; but in all cases the transferree pays the above-mentioned initiation fee of 2,000 gold dollars.

The prices for these seats vary, the fluctuations being due to the upward or downward trend of the stock market. Within recent years the price has risen considerably, and as much as 95,000 gold dollars has been paid to the transferrer. This is much higher than the price usually paid by new members in Stock Exchanges in Europe, yet when a seat becomes vacant there is no lack of purchasers. It is clear that a seat in the "House" is very valuable to the holder. In the building each member has a stall allotted to him where he has a telephone for his exclusive use; this enables him to communicate every transaction done in the Exchange to his business house, and to keep up connections with his constituents in other cities. When one of his constituents, say in Washington, D.C., desires to buy a certain security the order is conveyed to him direct, and executed without delay. I have seen a transaction of this kind executed in ten minutes, though there was a distance of several hundred miles between client and broker. The amount of business transacted in the "House" every day is enormous, aggregating many millions of dollars. New York also has other Exchanges, where different articles of merchandise are purchased and sold, such as corn, coffee, cotton, etc., and he volume of business transacted daily in that "Empire City" must be mmense, and almost beyond calculation.

Of course there are Exchanges in Chicago, Boston, Cincinnati, St. Louis, Philadelphia, Baltimore, Washington, and other cities, all conducted on similar lines, but the prices are always governed by the quotations from New York. This skilful and systematic way of doing business is remarkable, and I am inclined to believe that New York is ahead of many cities in South America and in Europe. No wonder that the services of Americans are required by other countries in industrial and technical concerns. Some years ago, when I was in Madrid, I noticed that the streetcar was running according to the American system, and upon inquiry I was told it was controlled by an American syndicate.

The pursuit of wealth in America is intense; it is apparent everywhere and seems to be the chief aim of the American people. Because of their eagerness to become rich as soon as possible they are all in a constant hurry. You may see people in the streets almost running to their offices, at luncheon they do not masticate their food, they bolt it, and in less than ten minutes are on their way back to their office again. Everyone is urged on by this spirit of haste, and you frequently hear of sudden deaths which doctors attribute to heart failure, or some other malady, but which I suspect are caused by the continual restless hurry and worry. People who are so unnaturally eager to get rich naturally suffer for it.

It is the general belief that Americans do not live as long as Europeans. They make money easily and their expectations are high. I have known many Americans who, in my opinion, were wealthy people, but they themselves did not think so; in fact, they said they were poor. Once I asked a gentleman, who was known to be worth half a million of gold dollars, whether it was not time for him to retire. He pooh-poohed the idea and said that he could not afford to give up his work. In reply to my inquiries he informed me that he would not call a man wealthy unless he should be possessed of one or two millions of dollars. With such extravagant ideas, it is no wonder that Americans work so hard. I grant that a man's mission in this world is to attain happiness. According to Webster, happiness is "that state of being which is attended with enjoyment," but it is curious to observe what different notions people have as to what happiness is. I know an Englishman in China who, by his skilful business management combined with good luck, has amassed immense wealth; in fact, he is considered the richest man in the port where he resides. He is a bachelor, over seventy years old, and leads a very simple life. But he still goes to his office every day, and toils as if he had to work for a living. Being told that he should discontinue his drudgery, as at his death he would have to leave his large fortune to relatives who would probably squander it, he gave an answer which is characteristic of the man. "I love," he said, "accumulating dollars and bank notes, and my enjoyment is in counting them; if my relatives who will inherit my fortune take as much pleasure in spending it as I have had in making it, they will be quite welcome to their joy." Not many people, I fancy, will agree with the old bachelor's view of life. I once suggested to a multi-millionaire of New York that it was time for him to retire from active work, leaving his sons to carry on his business. He told me that he would be unhappy without work and that he enjoyed the demands his business made on him each day.

Many a man's life has been shortened by his retiring from business. It is the mind rather than the body that lives, and apart from their business these men have no thoughts and therefore no life. A man's idea of happiness is greatly governed by his personal tastes, and is influenced by his environment, his education and the climate. The form which it is to assume may vary with persons of different tastes and positions, but it should not be carried out for his own benefit solely and it should not be injurious to his health or to his intellectual and spiritual improvement, nor should it be detrimental to the interests of other people.

7

American Freedom and Equality

When an Oriental, who, throughout his life, has lived in his own country where the will of his Sovereign is supreme and the personal liberty of the subject unknown, first sets foot on the soil of the United States, he breathes an atmosphere unlike anything he has ever known, and experiences curious sensations which are absolutely new. For the first time in his life he feels that he can do whatever he pleases without restraint, and that he can talk freely to people without fear. When he takes up a newspaper and reads statements about different persons in high positions which are not at all creditable to them, and learns that no serious consequences happen to the writers, he is lost in wonderment. After a little time he begins to understand that this is the "land of the free and the home of the brave", and that in America everybody is on an equality. The President, the highest official in the United States, is neither more nor less than a citizen; and should he, which is very unlikely, commit an offense, or do anything in contravention of the law, he would be tried in a Court of Justice in the same manner as the lowest and the poorest citizen. Naturally the new visitor thinks this the happiest people on earth, and wishes that his own country could be governed as happily. Until that lucky day arrives he feels that he would rather stay in free America than return to his native land.

One of the first lessons which is learned by the American child in school, and which is deeply impressed on its mind by its teacher, is that according to the Constitution all persons are born equal, and that no distinction is made between sections, classes, or sects.

No slaves, or persons under bonds, have been allowed in the United States since the abolition of slavery by President Lincoln. The moment a slave, or anyone in bonds, steps on the shores of the United States he is free, and no one, not even his former master, can deprive him of his liberty. America also affords an asylum for oppressed people and for political offenders; people who have been persecuted in their own land, on account of their religion or for political offenses, find a safe refuge in this country. Every year large numbers of Jews, and other foreigners, emigrate to America for the sake of enjoying religious freedom. Perfect religious liberty is guaranteed to everyone in the United States. There is equal religious liberty in England, but the King is compelled to belong to a particular section of the Christian Church, whereas in the United States no restriction is placed on the religious belief of the President; thus one President was a Baptist, another a Unitarian, and a third a Congregationalist; and, if elected, a Jew, a Mohammedan, or a Confucianist could become the President. Several Jews have held high Federal offices; they have even been Cabinet Ministers. Article VI of the Constitution of the United States says: "No religious test shall ever be required as a qualification to any office or public trust under the United States."

So ingrained in the minds of the American people is this principle of liberty and freedom of action that I do not believe they would resign it for any consideration whatsoever. Once an English Duke was asked whether he would accept the throne of China on the sole condition that he must reside in the Palace of Peking, and act as the Chinese Emperors have always been accustomed to act. He replied that such an exalted position of power and responsibility would be very great and tempting, but that he would on no account accept such an honor on such terms, as it would practically make him a prisoner. Though a subject under a monarchial form of government, he would not forfeit his right of freedom of action; and much less would a democratic American give up his birthright for any price. I knew an eminent and learned Judge of the Supreme Court in Washington, who used to say that he would never bend his knees to any human being, and that to the Almighty God alone would he ever do homage. He no doubt acted up to his principles, but I very much doubt if all Americans observe so lofty an ideal. A young lover in proposing to his sweetheart would not mind kneeling down to support his prayer. I have seen penitent husbands bending their knees to ask the forgiveness of their offended wives. This, however, can be explained by the fact that the act of kneeling is not, in such cases, a sign of inferiority, but the act of one equal asking a favor from another; still it is the bending of the knee which was so solemnly abjured by the learned Judge.

The dislike of distinction of classes which arises from the principle of equality is apparent wherever you go in the States. The railroad cars are not marked first, second, or third, as they are in Europe. It is true that there are Pullman cars, and palace cars, with superior and superb accommodation, and for which the occupant has to pay an extra fare; but the outside of the car simply bears the name "Pullman" without indicating its class, and anyone who is willing to pay the fare may share its luxuries. I should mention that in some of the Southern states negroes are compelled to ride on separate cars. On one occasion, arriving at the railroad station in one of those states, I noticed there were two waiting-rooms, one labelled "For the White", and the other "For the Colored." The railway porter took my portmanteau to the room for the white, but my conscience soon whispered I had come to the wrong place, as neither of the two rooms was intended for people of my complexion. The streetcars are more democratic; there is no division of classes; all people, high or low, sit in the same car without distinction of race, color or sex. It is a common thing to see a workman, dressed in shabby clothes full of dirt, sitting next to a millionaire or a fashionable lady gorgeously clothed. Cabinet officers and their wives do not think it beneath their dignity to sit beside a laborer, or a *coolie*, as he is called in China.

Foreign Ministers and Ambassadors coming to Washington soon learn to follow these local customs. In a European country they ride in coronated carriages, with two liverymen; but in Washington they usually go about on foot, or travel by the streetcars. I frequently saw the late Lord Pauncefote, the celebrated British Ambassador to Washington, ride to the State Department in the streetcar. My adoption of this democratic way of travelling during the time I was in America was the cause of a complaint being made against me at Peking. The complainants were certain Chinese high officials who had had occasion to visit the States; one of them had had a foreign education, and ought to have known better than to have joined in the accusation that my unpretentious manner of living was not becoming the dignity of a representative of China. They forgot that when in Rome you must do as the Romans do, and that to ride in a sumptuous carriage, with uniformed footmen, is in America not only an unnecessary expense, but a habit which, among such a democratic people as the Americans, would detract from, rather than add to, one's dignity. An envoy residing in a foreign country should be in touch with the people among whom he is sojourning. If he put on unnecessary airs, there will be a coldness and lack of cordiality between him and the community; his sphere of usefulness will be curtailed, and his knowledge of the people and their country limited. Of course, in a European capital, where every diplomat drives in a carriage, I should follow the example of my colleagues. But even in England I frequently met high statesmen, such, for example, as Lord Salisbury, walking in the streets. This unrestrained liberty and equality is remarkably conspicuous in the United States; for instance, at the White House official receptions or balls in Washington, I have seen ladies in ordinary dress, while on one occasion a woman appeared in the dress of a man. This was Doctor Mary Walker.

In a democratic country, such as the United States, one would naturally suppose that the people enjoyed a greater degree of freedom than is possible in monarchial countries. But, so far from this being so, in some respects, they appear to be in a worse position. On my return journey from South America, some years ago, our steamer had to stay for four hours outside of New York harbor. We had first to wait for the doctor to come on board to make his inspection of all the passengers, then the customs officials appeared and examined the luggage and boxes of all the passengers, and then, last but not the least, we had to wait for the immigration officers. All this necessarily took time, and it was not until all these inspections were completed that the steamer was allowed to enter the harbor, and to tie up alongside the dock. And this occurred in the land of freedom and liberty! I spoke to some of my American fellow passengers about the inconvenience and delay, and though they all murmured they quietly submitted. Customs and sanitary inspection should be so conducted as to cause as little delay as possible. I have visited many countries in Europe, in South America, and in Asia, but I have never known of a ship having to stay outside the harbor of the port of her destination for so long a time.

Take another case; some months since, I wished, in compliance with the request of a lady in America, to send her a Chow dog. A mutual friend was willing to take it to her, but, upon making inquiries at the American Consulate as to the Customs regulations, he was informed that it would be impossible for him to undertake the commission, as the Customs officers at San Francisco, besides imposing a heavy duty on the dog, would keep the ship in quarantine because the dog was on board. I could scarcely believe this, but inquiries confirmed the truth of my friend's statement. Customs and immigration laws and sanitary regulations must, of course, be observed, but they should be enforced in such a way as not to work hardship on the people. Officers entrusted with the performance of such duties, while faithfully and conscientiously performing their work, should yet exercise their power with discretion and tact. They are the servants of the people, and ought to look after their interests and convenience as well as after the interests of the State. I would be the last one to encourage smuggling, but would the national interests really suffer if the Custom House officers were to be a little more ready to accept a traveller's word, and if they were less ready to suspect everyone of making false declarations when entering the country? Smuggling must be repressed, but at the same time is it not true that the more imports enter the country the better it is for the State and for the people?

There are no peers in the United States, as the Government has no power to create them; and although America is nominally a free country, yet if a foreign government should confer a decoration on an American citizen for services rendered, he cannot accept it without the consent of Congress, just as under a monarchy a subject must obtain his sovereign's permission to wear a foreign decoration. It is true that there are some such titled persons in America, but they are not treated with any greater respect or distinction than other citizens; yet you frequently find people in America who not only would not disdain, but are actually anxious, to receive decorations from foreign governments. Once, at least, an American high official, just before leaving the country to which he had been accredited, accepted, without permission, a decoration, knowing that if he had asked for the consent of Congress he would not have been allowed to receive it.

It is human nature to love change and variety, and for every person to be designated "Mister" is too tame and flat for the go-ahead Americans. Hence many of the people whom you meet daily have some prefix to their names, such as General, Colonel, Major, President, Judge, etc. You will not be far wrong to call a man "Judge" when he is a lawyer; or "General" or "Colonel" if he has served in the army; or "Admiral" or "Captain" if he has been in the navy. Though neither the Federal nor the State Government has power to confer titles, the magnates do so. They see that dukes and other peers are created in Europe, and that the partners in the big, wealthy firms over there, are called "merchant princes," and so to outdo them, they arrogate to themselves a still higher title. Hence there are railroad kings, copper kings, tobacco kings, etc. It is, however, manifestly improper and incongruous that the people should possess a higher title than their President, who is the head of the nation. To make it even, I would suggest that the title "President" be changed to "Emperor," for the following reasons: First, it would not only do away with the impropriety of the chief magistrate of the nation assuming a name below that of some of his people, but it would place him on a level with the highest ruler of any nation on the face of the earth. I have often heard the remark that the President of the United States is no more than a common citizen, elected for four years, and that on the expiration of his term he reverts to his former humble status of a private citizen; that he has nothing in common with the dignified majesty of an Emperor; but were the highest official of the United States to be in future officially known as Emperor, all these depreciatory remarks would fall to the ground. There is no reason whatever why he should not be so styled, as, by virtue of his high office, he possesses almost as much power as the most aristocratic ruler of any nation. Secondly, it would clearly demonstrate the sovereign power of the people; a people who could make and unmake an Emperor would certainly be highly respected. Thirdly, the United States sends ambassadors to Germany, Austria, Russia, etc. According to international law, ambassadors have what is called the representative character, that is, they represent their sovereign by whom they are delegated, and are entitled to the same honors to which their constituent would be entitled were he personally present. In a republic where the head of the State is only a citizen and the sovereign is the people, it is only by a stretch of imagination that its ambassador can be said to represent the person of his sovereign. Now it would be much more in consonance with the dignified character of an American ambassador to be the representative of an Emperor than of a simple President. The name of Emperor may be distasteful to some, but may not a new meaning be given to it? A word usually has several definitions. Now, if Congress were to pass a law authorizing the chief magistrate of the United States of America to be styled Emperor, such designation to mean nothing more than the word "President", the title would soon be understood in that sense. There is no reason in history or philology why the word "Emperor" should never mean anything other than a hereditary ruler. I make this suggestion seriously, and hope it will be adopted.

Marriage laws in the United States, as I understand them, are more elastic than those in Europe. In England, until a few years ago, a man could not contract a legal marriage with his deceased wife's sister, although he could marry the betrothed wife of his deceased brother. It is curious to compare the Chinese view of these two cases. Marriage with a deceased wife's sister is, in China, not only lawful, but quite common, while to marry a dead brother's betrothed is strictly prohibited. Doubtless in the United States both are recognized as legal. I was not, however, prepared to hear, and when I did hear it, I could not at first believe that a man is permitted to marry his deceased son's wife. Let me quote from the "China Press," which has special facilities for obtaining news from America:

> Boston, March 24. The engagement of Mrs. Katherine M. B., widow of Charles A. B., and daughter of George C. F., chairman of the ...., Board of ...., to her father-in-law, Frank A. B., of ...., became known today. Charles A. B. was killed at the .... Road crossing in .... on March 29, 1910, by a locomotive which struck a carriage in which he was driving to the First Congregational Church, to serve as best man at the wedding of Miss H. R. F., another daughter of C. F., to L. G. B. of .... His wife, who was in the carriage with him and was to have been matron at the wedding, was severely injured. Her mother-in-law, Mrs. Frank A. B., died some months later.

I suppose the marriage has since been consummated. If a father is permitted to marry his deceased son's wife, in fairness a son should be allowed to marry his deceased father's wife. I presume that there is a law in the United States, or in some of the states, gainst marriages within the prohibited degrees of consanguinity and affinity, but I confess that the more I study the subject the more I am confused as to what is or what is not within the prohibited degrees.-

In China the law on this subject is extremely rigid, and consequently its infraction is exceedingly rare; I have, as a matter of fact, never heard of the marriage laws in China being broken. In "*Liao Chai*," a famous collection of Chinese tales, it is recorded that a young widow married her son and moved to another part of the country, so that their identity and relationship should be concealed. They seemed to have lived very happily together. After many years, when they had had children and grandchildren, their true relationship was accidentally discovered. A complaint was laid before the local authorities. After a long deliberation and careful review of the case, and to eradicate such "unnatural offspring," as they were termed, it was decided that the two offenders, and all their children and grandchildren should be burned to death, which sentence was duly carried out. I doubt if the story is authentic. It was probably fabricated by the author that it might serve as a warning. The sentence, if true, was too severe; the offspring who were innocent contributories to the crime deserved pity rather than punishment; the judgment passed on the real offenders was also unduly harsh. My object in citing this unsavory tale is to show the different views held in regard to incestuous marriage in China with its serious consequences.

It is commonly supposed that all men are born equal, and that the United States is the land of perfect equality. Now let us see if this is really so. There are men born into high stations of life, or into wealthy families, with "silver spoons" in their mouths; while there are others ushered into this world by parents who are paupers and who cannot support them. Then there are people born with wit and wisdom, while others are perfect fools. Again there are some who are brought to this life with strong and healthy constitutions, while others are weak and sickly. Thus it is plain that men are not born equal, either physically, intellectually, or socially. I do not know how my American friends account for this undoubted fact, but the Chinese doctrine of previous lives, of which the present are but the continuation, seems to afford a satisfactory explanation.

However, this doctrine of equality and independence has done immense good. It has, as a rule, caused men to think independently, and not to servilely follow the thoughts and ideas of others, who may be quite wrong. It has encouraged invention, and new discoveries in science and art. It has enabled men to develop industries and to expand trade. New York and Chicago, for example, could not have become such huge and prosperous cities within comparatively short periods, but for their free and wise institutions. In countries where personal liberty is unknown, and the rights of person and property are curtailed, people do not exert themselves to improve their environments, but are content to remain quiet and inactive.

By the constitution of the State of California it is declared that "all men are free and independent". It must be conceded that the American people enjoy a greater amount of freedom and independence than other people. But are they perfectly free, and are they really independent? Are they not swayed in politics by their "bosses", and do not many of them act and vote as their bosses dictate? In society are they not bound by conventionalities, and dare they infringe the strict rules laid down by the society leaders? In the matter of dress also are they not slaves, abjectly following new-fangled fashions imported from Paris? In domestic circles are not many husbands hen-pecked by their wives, because they, and not the men, rule the roost? Are not many women practically governed by their husbands, whose word is their law? The eager hunger for "the almighty dollar" leads most Americans to sacrifice their time, health, and liberty in the acquisition of wealth, and, alas, when they have acquired it, they find that their health is broken, and that they themselves are almost ready for the grave. Ought a free and independent people to live after this fashion?

In every well organized community it is essential that people should obey all laws and regulations which are enacted for the greatest good of the greatest number. In domestic circles they should willingly subordinate their own wishes to the wishes of others, for the sake of peace, concord and happiness. Happy that people whose laws and conditions are such that they can enjoy the greatest amount of freedom in regard to person and property, compatible with the general peace and good order of the community, and if I should be asked my opinion, notwithstanding all that I have above said concerning the United States, I should have to acknowledge that I believe that America is one of the few nations which have fairly well approximated the high ideal of a well-governed country.

Notes

* The names of the parties and places were given in full in the "China Press."

8

American Manners

Much has been written, and more said, about American manners, or rather the American *lack* of manners. Americans have frequently been criticized for their bad breeding, and many sarcastic references to American deportment have been made in my presence. I have even been told, I do not know how true it is, that European diplomats dislike being stationed in America, because of their aversion to the American way of doing things.

Much too has been written and said about Chinese manners, not only by foreigners but also by the Chinese. One of the classics, which our youth have to know by heart, is practically devoted entirely to manners. There has also been much adverse criticism of our manners or our excess of manners, though I have never heard that any diplomats have, on this account, objected to being sent to China. We Chinese are therefore in the same boat as the Americans. In regard to manners neither of us find much favor with foreigners, though for diametrically opposite reasons: the Americans are accused of observing too few formalities, and we of being too formal.

The Americans are direct and straight-forward. They will tell you to your face that they like you, and occasionally they also have very little hesitation in telling you that they do not like you. They say frankly just what they think. It is immaterial to them that their remarks are personal, complimentary or otherwise. I have had members of my own family complimented on their good looks as if they were children. In this respect Americans differ greatly from the English. The English adhere with meticulous care to the rule of avoiding everything personal. They are very much afraid of rudeness on the one hand, and of insincerity or flattery on the other. Even in the matter of such a harmless affair as a compliment to a foreigner on his knowledge of English, they will precede with a request for pardon, and speak in a half-apologetic manner, as if complimenting were something personal. The English and the Americans are closely related, they have much in common, but they also differ widely, and in nothing is the difference more conspicuous than in their conduct. I have, noticed curiously, enough that English Colonials, especially in such particulars as speech and manners, follow their *quondam* sister colony, rather than the mother country. And this, not only in Canada, where the phenomenon might be explained by climatic, geographic, and historic reasons, but also in such antipodean places as Australia and South Africa, which are so far away as to apparently have very little in common either with America or with each other. Nevertheless, whatever the reason, the transplanted Englishman, whether in the arctics or the tropics, whether in the Northern or the Southern Hemisphere, seems to develop a type quite different from the original stock, yet always resembling his fellow emigrants.

The directness of Americans is seen not only in what they say but in the way they say it. They come directly to the point without much preface or introduction, much less is there any circumlocution or "beating about the bush." When they come to see you they say their say and then take their departure, moreover they say it in the most terse, concise and unambiguous manner. In this respect what a contrast they are to us! We always approach each other with preliminary greetings. Then we talk of the weather, of politics or friends, of anything, in fact, which is as far as possible from the object of the visit. Only after this introduction do we broach the subject uppermost in our minds, and throughout the conversation polite courtesies are exchanged whenever the opportunity arises. These elaborate preludes and interludes may, to the strenuous, ever-in-a-hurry American, seem useless and superfluous, but they serve a good purpose. Like the common courtesies and civilities of life, they pave the way for the speakers, especially if they are strangers; they improve their tempers, and place them generally on terms of mutual understanding. It is said that some years ago a Foreign Consul in China, having a serious complaint to make on behalf of his national, called on the Taotai, the highest local authority in the port. He found the Chinese official so genial and polite that after half an hour's conversation, he advised the complainant to settle the matter amicably without troubling the Chinese officials about the matter. A good deal may be said in behalf of both systems. The American practice has at least the merit of saving time, an all important object with the American people. When we recall that this remarkable nation will spend millions of dollars to build a tunnel under a river, or to shorten a curve in a railroad, merely that they may save two or three minutes, we are not surprised at the abruptness of their speech. I, as a matter of fact, when thinking of their time-saving and abrupt manner of address, have been somewhat puzzled to account for that peculiar drawl of theirs. Very slowly and deliberately they enunciate each word and syllable with long-drawn emphasis, punctuating their sentences with pauses, some short and some long. It is almost an effort to follow a story of any length ~ the beginning often becomes cold before the end is reached. It seems to me that if Americans would speed up their speech after the fashion of their English cousins, who speak two or three times as quickly, they would save many minutes every day, and would find the habit not only more efficacious, but much more economical than many of their time-saving machines and tunnels. I offer this suggestion to the great American nation for what it is worth, and I know they will receive it in the spirit in which it is made, for they have the saving sense of humor.

Some people are ridiculously sensitive. Some years ago, at a certain place, a big dinner was given in honor of a notable who was passing through the district. A Chinese, prominent in local affairs, who had received an invitation, discovered that though he would sit among the honored guests, he would be placed below one or two whom he thought he ought to be above, and who, he therefore considered, would be usurping his rightful position. In disgust he refused to attend the dinner, which, excepting for what he imagined was a breach of manners, he would have been very pleased to have attended. Americans are much more sensible. They are not a bit sensitive, especially in small matters. Either they are broad-minded enough to rise above unworthy trifles, or else their good Americanism prevents their squabbling over questions of precedence, at the dinner table or elsewhere.

Americans act up to their Declaration of Independence, especially the principle it enunciates concerning the equality of man. They lay so much importance on this that they do not confine its application to legal rights, but extend it even to social intercourse. In fact, I think this doctrine is the basis of the so-called American manners. All men are deemed socially equal, whether as friend and friend, as President and citizen, as employer and employee, as master and servant, or as parent and child. Their relationship may be such that one is entitled to demand, and the other to render, certain acts of obedience, and a certain amount of respect, but outside that they are on the same level. This is doubtless a rebellion against all the social ideas and prejudices of the old world, but it is perhaps only what might be looked for in a new country, full of robust and ambitious manhood, disdainful of all traditions which in the least savor of monarchy or hierarchy, and eager to blaze as new a path for itself in the social,l as it has succeeded in accomplishing in the political, world. Combined with this is the American characteristic of saving time. Time is precious to all of us, but to Americans it is particularly so. We all wish to save time, but the Americans care much more about it than the rest of us. Then there are different notions about this question of saving time, different notions of what wastes time and what does not, and much which the Old World regards as politeness and good manners, Americans consider as a sheer waste of time. Time is, they think, far too precious to be occupied with ceremonies which appear empty and meaningless. It can, they say, be much more profitably filled with other and more useful occupations. In any discussion of American manners it would be unfair to leave out of consideration their indifference to ceremony and their highly developed sense of the value of time, but in saying this I do not forget that many Americans are devout ritualists, and that these find both comfort and pleasure in ceremony, which suggests that after all there is something to be said for the Chinese who have raised correct deportment almost to the rank of a religion.

The youth of America have not unnaturally caught the spirit of their elders, so that even children consider themselves as almost on a par with their parents, as almost on the same plane of equality; but the parents, on the other hand, also treat them as if they were equals, and allow them the utmost freedom. While a Chinese child renders unquestioning obedience to his parents' orders, such obedience as a soldier yields to his superior officer, the American child must have the whys and the wherefores duly explained to him, and the reason for his obedience made clear. It is not his parent that he obeys, but expediency and the dictates of reason. Here we see the clear-headed, sound, common-sense business man in the making.

The early training of the boy has laid the foundation for the future man. The child too has no compunction in correcting a parent even before strangers, and, what is stranger still, the parent accepts the correction in good part, and sometimes even with thanks. A parent is often interrupted in the course of a narrative, or discussion, by a small piping voice, setting right, or what it believes to be right, some date, place, or fact, and the parent, after a word of encouragement or thanks, proceeds. How different is our rule that a child is not to speak until spoken to! In Chinese official life under the old regime, it was not etiquette for one official to contradict another, especially when they were unequal in rank. When a high official expressed views which his subordinates did not endorse, they could not candidly give their opinion, but had to remain silent. I remember that some years ago some of my colleagues and I had an audience with a very high official, and when I expressed my dissent from some of the views of that high functionary, he rebuked me severely. Afterward he called me to him privately, and spoke to me somewhat as follows: "What you said just now was quite correct. I was wrong, and I will adopt your views, but you must not contradict me in the presence of other people. Do not do it again." There is, of course, much to be said for and against each system, and perhaps a blend of the two would give good results. Anyhow, we can trace in American customs that spirit of equality which pervades the whole of American society, and observe the germs of self-reliance and independence so characteristic of Americans, whether men, women, or children.

Even the domestic servant does not lose this precious American heritage of equality. I have nothing to say against that worthy individual, the American servant (if one can be found); on the contrary, none is more faithful or more efficient. But in some respects he is unique among the servants of the world. He does not see that there is any inequality between him and his master. His master, or should I say, his employer, pays him certain wages to do certain work, and he does it, but outside the bounds of this contract, they are still man and man, citizen and citizen. It is all beautifully, delightfully legal. The washerwoman is the "wash-lady," and is just as much a lady as her mistress. The word "servant" is not applied to domestics, "help" is used instead, very much in the same way that Canada and Australia are no longer English "colonies," but "self-governing dominions."

We of the Old World are accustomed to regard domestic service as a profession in which the members work for advancement, without much thought of ever changing their position. A few clever persons may ultimately adopt another profession, and, according to our antiquated conservative ways of thinking, rise higher in the social scale, but, for the large majority, the dignity of a butler or a housekeeper is the height of ambition, the crowning point in their career. Not so the American servant. Strictly speaking, there are no servants in America. The man, or the woman as the case may be, who happens for the moment to be your servant, is only a servant for the time being. He has no intention of making domestic service his profession, of being a servant for the whole of his life. To have to be subject to the will of others, even to the small extent to which American servants are subordinate, is offensive to an American's pride of citizenship, it is contrary to his conception of American equality. He is a servant only for the time, and until he finds something better to do. He accepts a menial position only as a stepping stone to some more independent employment. Is it to be wondered at that American servants have different manners from their brethren in other countries? When foreigners find that American servants are not like servants in their own country, they should not resent their behavior: it does not denote disrespect, it is only the outcrop of their natural independence and aspirations.

All titles of nobility are, by the Constitution, expressly forbidden. Even titles of honor or courtesy are but rarely used. "Honorable" is used to designate members of Congress; and for a few Americans, such as the President and the Ambassadors, the title "Excellency" is permitted. Yet, whether it is because the persons entitled to be so addressed do not think that even these mild titles are consistent with American democracy, or because the American public feels awkward in employing such stilted terms of address, they are not often used. I remember that on one occasion a much respected Chief Executive, on my proposing, in accordance with diplomatic usage and precedent, to address him as "Your Excellency," begged me to substitute instead "Mr. President." The plain, democratic "Mr." suits the democratic American taste much better than any other title, and is applied equally to the President of the Republic and to his coachman. Indeed the plain name John Smith, without even "Mr.", not only gives no offense, where some higher title might be employed, but fits just as well, and is in fact often used. Even prominent and distinguished men do not resent nicknames; for example, the celebrated person whose name is so intimately connected with that delight of American children and grown-ups - the "Teddy Bear." This characteristic, like so many other American characteristics, is due not only to the love of equality and independence, but also to the dislike of any waste of time.

In countries where there are elaborate rules of etiquette concerning titles and forms of address, none but a Master of Ceremonies can hope to be thoroughly familiar with them, or to be able to address the distinguished people without withholding from them their due share of high-sounding titles and epithets; and, be it whispered, these same distinguished people, however broad-minded and magnanimous they may be in other respects, are sometimes extremely sensitive in this respect. And even after one has mastered all the rules and forms, and can appreciate and distinguish the various nice shades which exist between "His Serene Highness," "His Highness," "His Royal Highness," and "His Imperial Highness," or between "Rt. Rev." and "Most Rev.", one has yet to learn what titles a particular person has, and with what particular form of address he should be approached, an impossible task even for a Master of Ceremonies, unless he always has in his pocket a *Burke's Peerage* to tell him who's who. What a waste of time, what an inconvenience, and what an unnecessary amount of irritation and annoyance all this causes. How much better to be able to address any person you meet simply as Mr. So-and-So, without unwittingly treading on somebody's sensitive corns! Americans have shown their common sense in doing away with titles altogether, an example which the sister republic of China is following. An illustrious name loses nothing for having to stand by itself without prefixes and suffixes, handles and tails. Mr. Gladstone was no less himself for not prefixing his name with Earl, and the other titles to which it would have entitled him, as he could have done had he not declined the so-called honor. Indeed, like the "Great Commoner," he, if that were possible, endeared himself the more to his countrymen because of his refusal. A name, which is great without resorting to the borrowed light of titles and honors, is greater than any possible suffix or affix which could be appended to it.

In conclusion, American manners are but an instance or result of the two predominant American characteristics to which I have already referred, and which reappear in so many other things American. A love of independence and of equality, early inculcated, and a keen abhorrence of waste of time, engendered by the conditions and circumstances of a new country, serve to explain practically all the manners and mannerisms of Americans. Even the familiar spectacle of men walking with their hands deep in their trouser pockets, or sitting with their legs crossed needs no other explanation, and to suggest that, because Americans have some habits which are peculiarly their own, they are either inferior or unmanly, would be to do them a grave injustice.

Few people are more warm-hearted, genial, and sociable than the Americans. I do not dwell on this, because it is quite unnecessary. The fact is perfectly familiar to all who have the slightest knowledge of them. Their kindness and warmth to strangers are particularly pleasant, and are much appreciated by their visitors. In some other countries, the people, though not unsociable, surround themselves with so much reserve that strangers are at first chilled and repulsed, although there are no pleasanter or more hospitable persons anywhere to be found when once you have broken the ice and learned to know them; but it is the stranger who must make the first advances, for they themselves will make no effort to become acquainted, and their manner is such as to discourage any efforts on the part of the visitor. You may travel with them for hours in the same car, sit opposite to them, and all the while they will shelter themselves behind a newspaper, the broad sheets of which effectively prohibit any attempts at closer acquaintance. The following instance, culled from a personal experience, is an illustration. I was a law student at Lincoln's Inn, London, where there is a splendid law library for the use of the students and members of the Inn. I used to go there almost every day to pursue my legal studies, and generally sat in the same quiet corner. The seat on the opposite side of the table was usually occupied by another law student. For months we sat opposite each other without exchanging a word. I thought I was too formal and reserved, so I endeavored to improve matters by occasionally looking up at him as if about to address him, but every time I did so he looked down as though he did not wish to see me. Finally I gave up the attempt. This is the general habit with English gentlemen. They will not speak to a stranger without a proper introduction; but in the case I have mentioned surely the rule would have been more honored by a breach than by the observance. Seeing that we were fellow students, it might have been presumed that we were gentlemen and on an equal footing. How different are the manners of the American! You can hardly take a walk, or go for any distance in a train, without being addressed by a stranger, and not infrequently making a friend. In some countries the fact that you are a foreigner only thickens the ice, but in America it thaws it. This delightful trait in the American character is also traceable to the same cause as that which has helped us to explain the other peculiarities which have been mentioned. To good Americans, not only are the citizens of America born equal, but the citizens of the world are also born equal.

9

American Women

It is rather bold on my part to take up this subject. It is a path where "fools rush in where angels fear to tread." No matter what I say it is sure to provoke criticism, but having frequently been asked by my lady friends to give my opinion of American women, and having given my solemn promise that if I ever should write my impressions of America I would do so, it would be a serious "breach of promise" if I should now break my word.

In general there are three classes of women: first, those who wish to be praised; secondly, those who wish to be adversely criticized and condemned; and thirdly, those who are simply curious to hear what others think of them. American women do not as a rule belong to either the first or the second class, but a large majority of them may be ranged under class three. They wish to know what other people honestly think of them and to hear their candid views. They are progressive people who desire to improve their defects whenever they are pointed out to them. That being the case I must not swerve from my duty of sitting in a high court of justice to pass judgment on them.

To begin with, the American women are in some respects dissimilar to the women of other nations. I find them sprightly, talkative and well informed. They can converse on any subject with ease and resource, showing that they have a good all-round education. Often have I derived considerable information from them. The persistence with which they stick to their opinions is remarkable. Once, when I had a lady visitor at my Legation in Washington, after several matters had been discussed we commenced talking about women's rights. I was in favor of giving women more rights than they are enjoying, but on some points I did not go so far as my lady friend; after arguing with me for several hours, she, seeing that I did not coincide with all her views, threatened that she would not leave my house until I had fully digested all her points, and had become converted to her views.

I have observed that many American women marry foreigners, but that an American rarely has a foreign wife. It may be said that foreigners marry American girls for their money, while American women marry distinguished foreigners for their titles. This may have been true in some cases, but other causes than such sordid motives must be looked for. It is the attractiveness and the beauty of the American girls which enable them to capture so many foreign husbands. Their pleasant manners and winsome nature predispose a person in their favor, and with their well-grounded education and ready fund of knowledge, they easily win any gentleman with marital propensities. Had I been single when I first visited America I too might have been a victim – no wonder then that American men prefer American wives. Once I was an involuntary match-maker. Some years ago, during my first mission in Washington, I was invited to attend the wedding of the daughter of the Chief Justice of the Supreme Court. When I entered the breakfast room, I saw the bridesmaids and a number of young men. Going up to one of the bridesmaids whom I had previously met, and who was the daughter of a Senator, I asked her when it would be her turn to become a bride. She modestly said that she did not know, as she had not yet had an offer. Turning to the group of young men who were in the room, I jocularly remarked to one of them, "This is a beautiful lady, would you not like to marry her?" He replied, "I shall be most delighted to." Then I said to the young lady, "Will you accept his offer?" She seemed slightly embarrassed and said something to the effect that as she did not know the gentleman she could not give a definite answer. After a few days I met the young lady at an "At Home" party when she scolded me for being so blunt with her before the young men. I told her I was actuated by the best of motives, and a few months later I received an invitation from the young lady's parents inviting me to be present at their daughter's marriage. I thought I would go and find out whether the bridegroom was the young man whom I had introduced to the young lady, and as soon as I entered the house, the mother of the bride, to my agreeable surprise, informed me that it was I who had first brought the young couple together, and both the bride and bridegroom heartily thanked me for my good offices.

One very conspicuous feature in the character of American women is their self-control and independence. As soon as a girl grows up she is allowed to do what she pleases, without the control of her parents. It is a common occurrence to see a young lady travelling alone without either a companion or a chaperon. Travelling on one occasion from San Francisco to Washington I met a young lady on the train who was still in her teens. She told me that she was going to New York to embark on a steamer for Germany, with the intention of entering a German college. She was undertaking this long journey alone. Such an incident would be impossible in China; even in England, or indeed in any European country, I hardly believe that a respectable young girl would be allowed to take such a journey without some trusty friend to look after her. But in America this is a common occurrence, and it is a credit to the administration, and speaks volumes for the good government of the country, that for sensible wide-awake American girls such undertakings are perfectly safe.

This notion of independence and freedom has modified the relation of children to their parents. Instead of children being required to show respect and filial obedience, the obligation of mutual love and esteem is cultivated. Parents would not think of ordering a girl or a boy to do anything, however reasonable; in all matters they treat them as their equals and friends; nor would a girl submit to an arbitrary order from her mother, for she does not

71

regard her as a superior, but as her friend and companion. I find it is a common practice among American girls to engage themselves in marriage without consulting their parents. Once I had a serious talk on this subject with a young couple who were betrothed. I asked them if they had the consent of their parents. They both answered emphatically that it was not necessary, and that it was their business and not their parents'. I told them that although it was their business, they might have shown some respect to their parents by consulting them before committing themselves to this important transaction. They answered that they did not agree with me, and as it concerned their own happiness alone, they had a perfect right to decide the matter for themselves. This shows the extreme limit to which the Americans carry their theory of independence. Unless I am greatly mistaken, I fear this is a typical and not an isolated case. I believe that in many cases, after they had made up their minds to marry, the young people would inform their respective parents of their engagement, but I question if they would subordinate their own wishes to the will of their parents, or ask their consent to their engagement.

Now let us see how all this is managed in China. Here the parties most interested have no voice in the matter. The parents, through their friends, or sometimes through professional match-makers, arrange the marriage, but only after the most strict and diligent inquiries as to the character, position, and suitability of temper and disposition of the persons for whom the marriage contract is being prepared. This is sometimes done with the knowledge of the interested parties, but very often they are not consulted. After an engagement is thus made it cannot be broken off, not even by the young people themselves, even though he or she may plead that the arrangement was made without his or her knowledge or consent. The engagement is considered by all parties as a solemn compact. On the wedding day, in nine cases out of ten, the bride and bridegroom meet each other for the first time, and yet they live contentedly, and quite often even happily together. Divorces in China are exceedingly rare. This is accounted for by the fact that, through the wise control of their parents, the children are properly mated. In saying this I do not wish to be supposed to be advocating the introduction of the Chinese system into America. I would, however, point out that the independent and thoughtless way in which the American young people take on themselves the marriage vow does not as a rule result in suitable companionships. When a girl falls in love with a young man she is unable to perceive his shortcomings and vices, and when, after living together for a few months, she begins to find them out, it is alas too late. If, previous to her engagement, she had taken her mother into her confidence, and asked her to use her good offices to find out the character of the young man whom she favored, a fatal and unhappy mistake might have been avoided. Without interfering, in the least, with their liberty or free choice, I should think it would be a good policy if all young Americans, before definitely committing themselves to a promise of marriage, would at least consult their mothers, and ask them to make private and confidential inquiries as to the disposition, as well as to the moral and physical fitness of the young man or lady whom they contemplate marrying. Mothers are naturally concerned about the welfare and happiness of their offspring, and could be trusted in most cases to make careful, impartial and conscientious inquiries as to whether the girl or man was really a worthy and suitable life partner for their children. If this step were generally taken many an unfortunate union would be avoided. It was after this fashion that I reasoned with the young people mentioned above, but they did not agree with me, and I had to conclude that love is blind.

Before leaving this subject I would add that the system of marriage which has been in vogue in China for so many centuries has been somewhat changed within the last few years. This is due to the new spirit which has been gradually growing. Young people begin to exert their rights, and will not allow parents to choose their life partners without their consent. Instances of girls choosing their own husbands have come to my knowledge, and they did not occur during leap-year. But I sincerely hope that our Chinese youth will not go to the same lengths as the young people of America.

The manner in which a son treats his parents in the United States is diametrically opposed to our Chinese doctrine, handed down to us from time immemorial. "Honor thy father and thy mother" is an injunction of Moses which all Christians profess to observe, but which, or so it appears to a Confucianist, all equally forget. The Confucian creed lays it down as the essential duty of children that they shall not only honor and obey their fathers and their mothers, but that they are in duty bound to support them. The reason is that as their parents brought them into the world, reared and educated them, the children should make them some return for their trouble and care. The view of this question which is taken in America seems to be very strange to me. Once I heard a young American argue in this way. He said, gravely and seriously, that as he was brought into this world by his parents without his consent, it was their duty to rear him in a proper way, but that it was no part of his duty to support them. I was very much astounded at this statement. In China such a son would be despised, and if he neglected to maintain his parents he would be punished. I do not believe that the extreme views of this young man are universally accepted in America, but I am inclined to think that the duties of children toward their parents are somewhat ill-defined. American parents do not apparently expect their children to support them, because as a rule they are, if not rich, at least in comfortable circumstances; and even if they are not, they would rather work for their livelihood than burden their children and hinder their success by relying on them for pecuniary aid. It may have escaped my observation, but, so far as I know, it is not the custom for young people to provide for their parents. There was, however, one exceptional case which came to my knowledge. Some years ago a young Senator in Washington, who was famous for his eloquence, had his father living with him. His father was eighty years of age and, though in robust health, was a cripple, and so had to depend on him for support. I was informed that he and his wife were very kind to him. Many young men treat their parents kindly and affectionately, but they do it more as a favor than as a duty; in fact, as between equals.

In connection with this subject I may mention that as soon as a son marries, however young and inexperienced he may be, he leaves his parents' roof. He and his bride will set up a separate establishment so that they can do as they please without the supervision of their parents. The latter do not object, as it gives the young folk an opportunity to gain experience in keeping house. Young wives have a horror of having their mothers-in-law reside with them; if it be necessary to have an elderly lady as a companion they always endeavor to get their own mothers.

American women are ambitious and versatile, and can readily apply themselves to any task with ease. They are not only employed in stores and mercantile houses, but are engaged in different professions. There is scarcely any store in America where there are not some women employed as typists, clerks, or accountants. I am told that they are more steady than men. Even in the learned professions they successfully compete with the men. Some years ago the Attorney-Generalship of one of the states became vacant. Two candidates appeared; one was a gentleman and the other a young lady lawyer. They both sought election; the gentleman secured a small majority, but in the end the lady lawyer conquered, for she soon became the wife of the Attorney-General, her former opponent during the election campaign, and after her marriage she practically carried on the work of her husband. Some years later her husband retired from practice in order to farm, and she continued to carry on the law practice. Does not this indicate that the intellect of the American woman is equal, if not superior, to that of the men? American women are good conversationalists, and many of them are eloquent and endowed with "the gift of the gab." One of the cleverest and wittiest speeches I have ever heard was from a woman who spoke at a public meeting on a public question. They are also good writers. Such women as Mrs. Ella Wheeler Wilcox, Mrs. Mary N. Foote Henderson, Mrs. Elizabeth Towne, and many others, are a great credit to their sex. The writings of such women show their profound insight and wide culture. Naturally such women cannot be expected to play second fiddle. They exercise great influence, and when married "they rule the roost." It should be mentioned that their husbands submit willingly to their tactful rule, and gladly obey their commands without feeling that they are servants. I would advise any married woman who complains of her husband being unruly and unpleasant to take a lesson from the ladies of America. They are vivacious, bright, loquacious and less reserved than European ladies. In social functions they can be easily recognized. If, however, an American lady marries a foreigner and lives abroad, she soon loses her national characteristics. Once on board a steamer I had an American lady as a fellow passenger; from her reserved manner I mistook her for an English lady, and it was only after some days that I discovered she was born in

America, but that she had been living in England for many years with her English husband.

There is one fault I find with American women, if it can be so called, and that is their inquisitiveness; I know that this is a common fault with all women, but it is most conspicuous in the Americans. They have the knack of finding out things without your being aware of it, and if they should want to know your history they will learn all about it after a few minutes' conversation. They are good detectives, and I think they should be employed in that line more than they are.

A nation's reputation depends upon the general character of its women, for they form at least half, if not more, of the population. In this respect America stands high, for the American woman is lively, open-hearted and ingenuous; she is also fearless, independent, and is almost without restraint. She is easily accessible to high and low, and friendly to all, but woe to the man who should misunderstand the pure and high character of an American girl, and attempt to take liberties with her. To a stranger, and especially to an Oriental, she is a puzzle. Some years ago I had to disabuse the false notion of a countryman of mine respecting a lady's behavior toward him. The keen observer will find that the American girl, having been educated in schools and colleges with boys, naturally acts more freely than her sisters in other countries, where great restraint is imposed upon them. Her actions may be considered as perilously near to the border of masculinity, yet she is as far from either coarseness or low thoughts as is the North from the South Pole. The Chinese lady is as pure as her American sister, but she is brought up in a different way; her exclusion keeps her indoors, and she has practically no opportunity of associating with male friends. A bird which has been confined in a cage for a long time, will, when the door is opened, fly far away and perhaps never return, but if it has been tamed and allowed to go in and out of its cage as it pleases it will not go far, but will always come back in the evening. When my countrywomen are allowed more freedom they will not abuse it, but it will take some little time to educate them up to the American standards.

10

American Costumes

Fashion is the work of the devil. When he made up his mind to enslave mankind he found in fashion his most effective weapon. Fashion enthralls man, it deprives him of his freedom; it is the most autocratic dictator, its mandate being obeyed by all classes, high and low, without exception. Every season it issues new decrees, and no matter how ludicrous they are, everyone submits forthwith. The fashions of this season are changed in the next. Look, for example, at women's hats; some years ago the "merry widow," which was about two or three feet in diameter, was all the rage, and the larger it became, the more fashionable it was. Sometimes the wearer could hardly go through a doorway. Then came the hat crowned with birds' feathers, some ladies even placing the complete bird on their hats ~ a most ridiculous exhibition of bad taste. The Society for the Prevention of Cruelty to Animals should take up the question of the destruction of birds for their plumage, and agitate until the law makes it illegal to wear a bird on a hat. Some may say that if people kill animals and birds for food they might just as well wear a dead bird on their hats, if they wish to be so silly, although the large majority of America's population, I am sorry to find, sincerely believe meat to be a necessary article of diet; yet who will claim that a dead bird on a hat is an indispensable article of wearing apparel? Why do we dress at all? First, I suppose, for protection against cold and heat; secondly, for comfort; thirdly, for decency; and, fourthly, for ornament. Now does the dress of Americans meet these requirements?

First, as regards the weather, does woman's dress protect her from the cold? The fact that a large number of persons daily suffer from colds arouses the suspicion that their dress is at fault. The body is neither equally nor evenly covered, the upper portion being as a rule nearly bare, or very thinly clad, so that the slightest exposure to a draught, or a sudden change of temperature, subjects the wearer to the unpleasant experience of catching cold, unless she is so physically robust and healthy that she can resist all the dangers to which her clothing, or rather her lack of clothing, subjects her. Indeed ladies' dress, instead of affording protection, sometimes endangers their lives. The following extract from the "London Times" - and the facts cannot be doubted - is a warning to the fair sex:

> "The strong gale which swept over Bradford resulted in an extraordinary accident by which a girl lost her life. Mary Bailey, aged 16, the daughter of an electrician, who is a pupil at the Hanson Secondary School, was in the school yard when she was suddenly lifted up into the air by a violent gust of wind which got under her clothes converting them into a sort of parachute. After being carried to a height estimated by spectators at 20 feet, she turned over in the air and fell to the ground striking the concreted floor of the yard with great force. She was terribly injured and died half an hour later."

Had the poor girl been wearing Chinese clothing this terrible occurrence could not have happened; her life would not have been sacrificed to fashion.

As to the second point, comfort, I do not believe that the wearer of a fashionable costume is either comfortable or contented. I will say nothing of the unnecessary garments which the average woman affects, but let us see what can be said for the tight corset binding the waist. So far from being comfortable it must be most inconvenient, a sort of perpetual penance, and it is certainly injurious to the health. I feel confident that physicians will support me in my belief that the death-rate among American women would be less if corsets and other tight lacing were abolished. I have known of instances where tight lacing for the ballroom has caused the death of *enceinte* women.

As to the third object, decency, I am not convinced that the American dress fulfils this object. When I say American dress, I include also the clothing worn by Europeans, for both are practically the same. It may be a matter of education, but from the Oriental point of view we would prefer that ladies' dresses should be worn more loosely, so that the figure should be less prominent. I am aware that this is a view which my American friends do not share. It is very curious that what is considered as indecent in one country is thought to be quite proper in another. During the hot summers in the Province of Kiangsu the working women avoid the inconveniences and chills of perspiration by going about their work with nothing on the upper part of their bodies, except a chest protector to cover the breasts; in Western countries women would never think of doing this, even during a season of extreme heat; yet they do not object, even in the depth of winter, to uncovering their shoulders as low as possible when attending a dinner-party, a ball, or the theater. I remember the case of a Chinese rice-pounder in Hongkong who was arrested and taken to the Police Court on a charge of indecency. To enable him to do his work better he had dispensed with all his clothing excepting a loin cloth; for this he was sentenced to pay a fine of $2, or, in default of payment, to be imprisoned for a week. The English Magistrate, in imposing the fine, lectured him severely, remarking that in a civilized community such primitive manners could not be tolerated, as they were both barbarous and indecent. When he said this did he think of the way the women of his country dress when they go to a ball?

It must be remembered that modesty is wholly a matter of conventionality and custom. Competent observers have testified that savages who have been accustomed to nudity all their lives are covered with shame when made to put on clothing for the first time. They exhibit as much confusion as a civilized person would if compelled to strip naked in public. In the words of a competent authority on this subject: "The facts appear to prove that the feeling of shame, far from being the cause of man's covering his body is, on the contrary, a result of this custom; and that the covering, if not used as a protection from the climate, owes its origin, at least in many cases, to the desire of men and women to make themselves attractive." Strange as it may seem, it is nevertheless true that a figure partially clad appears more indecent than one that is perfectly nude.

The fourth object of clothes is ornament, but ornaments should be harmless, not only to the wearer, but also to other people; yet from the following paragraph, copied from one of the daily newspapers, it does not appear that they are:

London, May 7. The death of a girl from blood-poisoning caused by a hatpin penetrating her nose was inquired into at Stockport, Cheshire, yesterday. The deceased was Mary Elizabeth Thornton, aged twenty-four, daughter of a Stockport tradesman. The father said that on Saturday evening, April 20, his daughter was speaking to a friend, Mrs. Pickford, outside the shop. On the following Monday she complained of her nose being sore. Next day she again complained and said, "It must be the hatpin." While talking to Mrs. Pickford, she explained, Mrs. Pickford's baby stumbled on the footpath. They both stooped to pick it up, and a hatpin in Mrs. Pickford's hat caught her in the nostril. His daughter gradually got worse and died on Saturday last. Mrs. Pickford, wife of a paper merchant, said that some minutes after the deceased had picked up the child she said, "Do you know, I scratched my nose on your hatpin?" Mrs. Pickford was wearing the hatpin in court. It projected two inches from the hat and was about twelve inches in length. Dr. Howie Smith said that septic inflammation was set up as a result of the wound, and, travelling to the brain, caused meningitis.The coroner said that not many cases came before coroners in which death was directly traceable to the hatpin but there must be a very large number of cases in which the hatpin caused injury, in some cases loss of sight. It was no uncommon sight to see these deadly weapons protruding three or four inches from the hat. In Hamburg women were compelled by statute to put shields or protectors on the points of hatpins. In England nothing had been done, but this case showed that it was high time something was done. If women insisted on wearing hatpins they should take precaution of wearing also a shield or protector which would prevent them inflicting injury on other people. The jury returned a verdict of accidental death, and expressed their opinion that long hatpins ought to be done away with or their points protected.

To wear jewels, necklaces of brilliants, precious stones and pearls, or ribbons with brilliants round the hair is a pleasing custom and a pretty sight. But to see a lady wearing a long gown trailing on the ground does not impress me as being elegant, though I understand the ladies in Europe and America think otherwise. It would almost seem as if their conceptions of beauty depended on the length of their skirts. In a ballroom one sometimes finds it very difficult not to tread on the ladies' skirts, and on ceremonial occasions each lady has two page boys to hold up the train of her dress. It is impossible to teach an Oriental to appreciate this sort of thing. Certainly skirts which are not made either for utility or comfort, and which fashion changes, add nothing to the wearer's beauty; especially does this remark apply to the "hobble skirt," with its impediment to free movement of the legs. The ungainly "hobble skirt" compels the wearer to walk carefully and with short steps, and when she dances she has to lift up her dress. Now the latest fashion seems to be the "slashed skirt" which, however, has the advantage of keeping the lower hem of the skirt clean. Doubtless this, in turn, will give place to other novelties. A Chinese lady, Doctor Ya Mei-kin, who has been educated in America, adopted while there the American attire, but as soon as she returned to China she resumed her own native dress. Let us hear what she has to say on this subject. Speaking of Western civilization she said: "If we keep our own mode of life it is not for the sake of blind conservatism. We are more logical in our ways than the average European imagines. I wear for instance this 'ao' dress as you see, cut in one piece and allowing the limbs free play - because it is manifestly a more rational and comfortable attire than your fashionable skirt from Paris. On the other hand we are ready to assimilate such notions from the West as will really prove beneficial to us." Beauty is a matter of education: when you have become accustomed to anything, however quaint or queer, you will not think it so after a while. When I first

81

went abroad and saw young girls going about in the streets with their hair falling loose over their shoulders, I was a little shocked. I thought how careless their parents must be to allow their girls to go out in that untidy state. Later, finding that it was the fashion, I changed my mind, until by degrees I came to think that it looked quite nice; thus do conventionality and custom change one's opinions. But it should be remembered that no custom or conventionality which sanctions the distorting of nature, or which interferes with the free exercise of any member of the body, can ever be called beautiful. It has always been a great wonder to me that American and European ladies, who are by no means slow to help forward any movement for reform, have taken no active steps to improve the uncouth and injurious style of their own clothes. How can they expect to be granted the privileges of men until they show their superiority by freeing themselves from the enthrallment of the conventionalities of fashion?

Men's dress is by no means superior to the women's. It is so tight that it causes the wearer to suffer from the heat much more than is necessary, and I am certain that many cases of sunstroke have been chiefly due to tight clothing. I must admire the courage of Dr. Mary Walker, an American lady, who has adopted man's costume, but I wonder that, with her singular independence and ingenuity, she has not introduced a better form of dress, instead of slavishly adopting the garb of the men. I speak from experience. When I was a law student in England, in deference to the opinion of my English friends, I discarded Chinese clothes in favor of the European dress, but I soon found it very uncomfortable. In the winter it was not warm enough, but in summer it was too warm because it was so tight. Then I had trouble with the shoes. They gave me the most distressing corns. When, on returning to China, I resumed my own national costume my corns disappeared, and I had no more colds. I do not contend that the Chinese dress is perfect, but I have no hesitation in affirming that it is more comfortable and, according to my views, very much prettier than the American fashions. It is superior to any other kind of dress that I have known. To appreciate the benefits to be derived from comfortable clothing, you have to wear it for a while. Dress should not restrain the free movement of every part of the body, neither should it be so tight as to hinder in any way the free circulation of the blood, or to interfere with the process of evaporation through the skin. I cannot understand why Americans, who are correct and cautious about most things, are so very careless of their own personal comfort in the matter of clothing. Is anything more important than that which concerns their health and comfort? Why should they continue wearing clothes which retard their movements, and which are so inconvenient that they expose the wearers to constant risk and danger? How can they consistently call themselves independent while they servilely follow the mandates of the dressmakers who periodically make money by inventing new fashions necessitating new clothes? Brave Americans, wake up! Assert your freedom!

It would be very bold, and indeed impertinent, on my part to suggest to my American friends that they should adopt the Chinese costume. It has much to recommend it, but I must candidly confess that it might be improved. Why not convene an international congress to decide as to the best form of dress for men and women? Male and female delegates from all over the world might be invited, and samples of all kinds of costumes exhibited. Out of them all let those which are considered the best for men and most suitable for women be recommended, with such improvements as the congress may deem necessary. The advantages of a universal uniformity of costumes would be far-reaching. There would be no further occasion for any one to look askance at another, as has frequently happened when some stranger has been seen wearing what was considered an uncomely or unsuitable garb; universal uniformity of costume would also tend to draw people closer together, and to make them more friendly. Uniforms and badges promote brotherhood. I have enough faith in the American people to believe that my humble suggestion will receive their favorable consideration, and that in due time it will be carried into effect.

11

American versus Chinese Civilization

This is a big subject. Its exhaustive treatment would require a large volume. In a little chapter such as this I have no intention of doing more than to cast a glance at its cuff buttons and some of the frills on its shirt. Those who want a thesis must look elsewhere.

Now what is Civilization? According to Webster it is "the act of civilizing or the state of being civilized; national culture; refinement." "Civilization began with the domestication of animals," says Alfred Russell Wallace, but whether for the animal that was domesticated or for the man domesticating it is not clear. In a way the remark probably applies to both, for the commencement of culture, or the beginning of civilization, was our reclamation from a savage state. Burke says: "Our manners, our civilization, and all the good things connected with manners and civilization have in this European world of ours depended for ages upon two principles ~ the spirit of a gentleman, and the spirit of religion." We often hear people, especially Westerners, calling themselves "highly civilized," and to some extent they have good grounds for their claim, but do they really manifest the qualifications mentioned by Burke? Are they indeed so "highly civilized" as to be in all respects worthy paragons to the so-called semi-civilized nations? Have not some of their policies been such as can be characterized only as crooked and selfish actions which less civilized peoples would not have thought of? I believe that every disinterested reader will be able to supply confirmatory illustrations for himself, but I will enforce the point by giving a few Chinese ideals of a truly civilized man:

"He guards his body as if holding jade" - i.e., he will not contaminate himself with mental or moral filth.

"He does not gratify his appetite, nor in his dwelling place does he seek ease" - i.e., he uses the physical without being submerged by it.

"Without weapons he will not attack a tiger, nor will he dare to cross a river without a boat" - in other words, he will never ruin himself and his family by purely speculative practices.

He will "send charcoal in a snowstorm, but he will not add flowers to embroidery" - meaning that he renders timely assistance when necessary, but does not curry favor by presents to those who do not need them.

Our most honored heroes are said to have made their virtue "brilliant" and one of them engraved on his bath-tub the axiom - "If you can renovate yourself one day, do so from day to day. Let there be daily renovation." Our ideal for the ruler is that the regulation of the state must commence with his regulation of himself.

It is too often forgotten that civilization, like religion, originally came from the East. Long before Europe and America were civilized, yea while they were still in a state of barbarism, there were nations in the East, including China, superior to them in manners, in education, and in government; possessed of a literature equal to any, and of arts and sciences totally unknown in the West. Self-preservation and self-interest make all men restless, and so Eastern peoples gradually moved to the West, taking their knowledge with them; Western people who came into close contact with them learned their civilization. This fusion of East and West was the beginning of Western civilization.

A Chinese proverb compares a pupil who excels his teacher to the color green, which originates from blue, but is superior to it. This may aptly be applied to Westerners, for they originally learned literature, science, and other arts from the East; but they have proven apt pupils and have excelled their old masters. I wish I could find an apothegm concerning a former master who went back to school and surpassed his clever pupil. The non-existence of such a maxim probably indicates that no such case has as yet occurred, but that by no means proves that it never will.

Coming now to particulars, I would say that one of the distinguishing features in the American people which I much admire is their earnestness and perseverance. When they decide to take up anything, whether it be an invention or the investigation of a difficult problem, they display indomitable perseverance and patience. Mr. Edison, for example, sleeps, it is said, in his factory, and is inaccessible for days when he has a problem to solve, frequently even forgetting food and sleep. I can only compare him to our sage Confucius, who, hearing a charming piece of music which he wanted to study, became so engrossed in it that for many days he forgot to eat, while for three months he did not know the taste of meat.

The dauntless courage of the aviators, not only in America, but in Europe also, is a wonderful thing. "The toll of the air," in the shape of fatal accidents from aviation, mounts into the hundreds, and yet men are undeterred in the pursuit of their investigations. With such intrepidity, perseverance, and genius, it is merely a question of time, and I hope it will not be long, until the art of flying, either by aeroplanes or airships, will be perfectly safe. When that time arrives I mean to make an air trip to America, and I anticipate pleasures from the novel experience such as I do not get from travelling by land or sea.

The remarkable genius for organization observable anywhere in America arouses the visitor's enthusiastic admiration. One visits a mercantile office where a number of men are working at different desks in a large room, and marvels at the quiet and systematic manner in which they perform their tasks;

or one goes to a big bank and is amazed at the large number of customers ever going in and coming out. It is difficult to calculate the enormous amount of business transacted every hour, yet all is done with perfect organization and a proper division of labor, so that any information required is furnished by the manager or by a clerk, at a moment's notice. I have often been in these places, and the calm, quiet, earnest way in which the employees performed their tasks was beyond praise. It showed that the heads who organized and were directing the institutions had a firm grasp of multiplex details.

We Chinese have a reputation for being good business men. When in business on our own account, or in partnership with a few friends, we succeed marvelously well; but we have yet much to learn regarding large concerns such as corporations or joint stock companies. This is not to be wondered at, for joint stock companies and corporations as conducted in the West were unknown in China before the advent of foreign merchants in our midst. Since then a few joint stock companies have been started in Hong Kong, Shanghai, and other ports; these have been carried on by the Chinese exclusively, but the managers have not as yet mastered the systematic Western methods of conducting such concerns. Even unpractised and inexpert eyes can see great room for improvement in the management of these businesses. Here, I must admit, the Japanese are ahead of us. Take, for instance, the Yokohama Specie Bank: it has a paid-up capital of Yen 30,000,000 and has branches and agencies not only in all the important towns in Japan, but also in different ports in China, London, New York, San Francisco, Honolulu, Bombay, Calcutta and other places. It is conducted in the latest and most approved scientific fashion; its reports and accounts, published half-yearly, reveal the exact state of the concern's financial position and, incidentally, show that it makes enormous profits. True, several Chinese banks of a private or official nature have been established, and some of them have been doing a fair business, but candor compels me to say that they are not conducted as scientifically as is the Yokohama Specie Bank, or most American banks. Corporations and joint stock companies are still in their infancy in China; but Chinese merchants and bankers, profiting by the mistakes of the past, will doubtless gradually improve their systems, so that in the future there will be less and less cause to find fault with them.

One system which has been in vogue within the last ten or twenty years in America, and which has lately figured much in the limelight, is that of "Trusts." Here, again, it is only the ingenuity of Americans which could have brought the system to such gigantic proportions as to make it possible for it to wield an immense influence over trade, not only in America but in other countries also. The main object of the Trust seems to be to combine several companies under one direction, so as to economize expenses, regulate production and the price of commodities by destroying competition. Its advocates declare their policy to be productive of good to the world, inasmuch as it secures regular supplies of commodities of the best kind at fair and reasonable prices. On the other hand, its opponents contend that Trusts are injurious to the real interests of the public, as small companies cannot compete with them, and without healthy competition the consumer always suffers. Where experts differ it were perhaps wiser for me not to express an opinion lest I should show no more wisdom than the boy who argued that lobsters were black and not red because he had often seen them swimming about on the seashore, but was confuted by his friend who said he knew they were red and not black for he had seen them on his father's dinner table.

The fact, however, which remains indisputable, is the immense power of wealth. No one boycotts money. It is something no one seems to get enough of. I have never heard that multi-millionaires like Carnegie or Rockefeller ever expressed regrets at not being poor, even though they seem more eager to give money away than to make it. Most people in America are desirous for money, and rush every day to their business with no other thought than to accumulate it quickly. Their love of money leaves them scarcely time to eat, to drink, or to sleep; waking or sleeping they think of nothing else. Wealth is their goal and when they reach it they will probably be still unsatisfied. The Chinese are, of course, not averse to wealth. They can enjoy the jingling coin as much as anyone, but money is not their only thought. They carry on their business calmly and quietly, and they are very patient. I trust they will always retain these habits and never feel any temptation to imitate the Americans in their mad chase after money.

There is, however, one American characteristic my countrymen might learn with profit, and that is the recognition of the fact that punctuality is the soul of business. Americans know this; it is one cause of their success. Make an appointment with an American and you will find him in his office at the appointed time. Everything to be done by him during the course of the day has its fixed hour, and hence he is able to accomplish a greater amount of work in a given time than many others. The Chinese, unfortunately, have no adequate conceptions of the value of time. This is due, perhaps, to our mode of reckoning. In the West a day is divided into twenty-four hours, and each hour into sixty minutes, but in China it has been for centuries the custom to divide day and night into twelve "periods" of two hours each, so that an appointment is not made for a particular minute, as in America, but for one or other of these two-hour periods. This has created ingrained habits of unpunctuality, which clocks and watches and contact with foreigners are slow to remove. The time-keeping railway is, however, working a revolution, especially in places where there is only one train a day, and a man who misses that has to wait for the morrow before he can resume his journey.

Some years ago a luncheon - "tiffin" we call it in China - was given in my honor at a Peking restaurant by a couple of friends; the hour was fixed at noon sharp. I arrived on the stroke of twelve, but found that not only were none of the guests there, but that even the hosts themselves were absent. As I had several engagements I did not wait, but I ordered a few dishes and ate what I required. None of the hosts had made their appearance by the time I had finished, so I left with a request to the waiter that he would convey my thanks.

Knowing the unpunctuality of our people, the conveners of a public meeting will often tell the Chinese that it will begin an hour or two before the set time, whereas foreigners are notified of the exact hour. Not being aware of this device I once attended a conference at the appointed time, only to find that I had to wait for over an hour. I protested that in future I should be treated as a foreigner in this regard.

As civilized people have always found it necessary to wear clothes I ought not to omit a reference to them here, but in view of what has already been said in the previous chapter I shall at this juncture content myself with quoting Mrs. M. S. G. Nichols, an English lady who has written on this subject. She characterizes the clothing of men as unbeautiful, but she principally devotes her attention to the dress of women. I quote the following from her book:[*]

> The relation of a woman's dress to her health is seldom considered, still less is it contemplated as to its effect upon the health of her children; yet everyone must see that all that concerns the mothers of our race is important. The clothing of woman should be regarded in every aspect if we wish to see its effect upon her health, and consequently upon the health of her offspring. The usual way is to consider the beauty or fashion of dress first, its comfort and healthfulness afterward, if at all. We must reverse this method. First, use; then beauty, flowing from, or in harmony with, use. That is the true law of life.
>
> (p.14)

On page 23 she continues: "A great deal more clothing is worn by women in some of fashion's phases than is needed for warmth, and mostly in the form of heavy skirts dragging down upon the hips. The heavy trailing skirts also are burdens upon the spine. Such evils of women's clothes, especially in view of maternity, can hardly be over-estimated. The pains and perils that attend birth are heightened, if not caused, by improper clothing. The nerves of the spine and the maternal system of nerves become diseased together." And on page 32 she writes: "When I first went to an evening party in a fashionable town, I was shocked at seeing ladies with low dresses, and I cannot even now like to see a man, justly called a rake, looking at the half-exposed bosom of a lady. There is no doubt that too much clothing is an evil, as well as too little; but clothing that swelters or leaves us with a cold are both lesser evils than the exposure of esoteric charms to stir the already heated blood of the *roue*. What we have to do, as far as fashion and the public opinion it forms will allow, is to suit our clothing to our climate, and to be truly modest and healthful in our attire."

Mrs. Nichols, speaking from her own experience, has naturally devoted her book largely to a condemnation of woman's dress, but man's dress as worn in the West is just as bad. The dreadful high collar and tight clothes which are donned all the year round, irrespective of the weather, must be very uncomfortable. Men wear nearly the same kind of clothing at all seasons of the year. That might be tolerated in the frigid or temperate zones, but should not the style be changed in the tropical heat of summer common to the Eastern countries? I did not notice that men made much difference in their dress in summer; I have seen them, when the thermometer was ranging between 80 and 90, wearing a singlet shirt, waistcoat and coat. The coat may not have been as thick as that worn in winter, still it was made of serge, wool or some similarly unsuitable stuff. However hot the weather might be it was seldom that anyone was to be seen on the street without a coat. No wonder we frequently hear of deaths from sunstroke or heat, a fatality almost unknown among the Chinese.**

Chinese dress changes with the seasons, varying from the thickest fur to the lightest gauze. In winter we wear fur or garments lined with cotton wadding; in spring we don a lighter fur or some other thinner garment; in summer we use silk, gauze or grass cloth, according to the weather. Our fashions are set by the weather; not by the arbitrary decrees of dressmakers and tailors from Peking or elsewhere. The number of deaths in America and in Europe every year resulting from following the fashion must, I fear, be considerable, although of course no doctor would dare, in his death certificate, to assign unsuitable clothing as the cause of the decease of a patient.

Even in the matter of dressing, and in this twentieth century, "might is right." In the opinion of an impartial observer the dress of man is queer, and that of woman, uncouth; but as all nations in Europe and America are wearing the same kind of dress, mighty Conventionality is extending its influence, so that even some natives of the East have discarded their national dress in favor of the uglier Western attire. If the newly adopted dress were, if no better than, at least equal to the old one in beauty and comfort, it might be sanctioned for the sake of uniformity, as suggested in the previous chapter; but when it is otherwise why should we imitate? Why should the world assume a depressing monotony of costume? Why should we allow nature's diversities to disappear? Formerly a Chinese student when returning from Europe or America at once resumed his national dress, for if he dared to continue to favor the Western garb he was looked upon as a "half-foreign devil." Since the establishment of the Chinese Republic in 1911, this sentiment has entirely changed, and the inelegant foreign dress is no longer considered fantastic; on the contrary it has become a fashion, not only in cities where foreigners are numerous, but even in interior towns and villages where they are seldom seen.

Chinese ladies, like their Japanese sisters, have not yet, to their credit be it said, become obsessed by this new fashion, which shows that they have more common sense than some men. I have, however, seen a few young and foolish girls imitating the foreign dress of Western women. Indeed this craze for Western fashion has even caught hold of our legislators in Peking, who, having fallen under the spell of clothes, in solemn conclave decided that the frock coat, with the tall-top hat, should in future be the official uniform; and the swallow-tail coat with a white shirt front the evening dress in China. I need hardly say that this action of the Peking Parliament aroused universal surprise and indignation. How could the scholars and gentry of the interior, where foreign tailors are unknown, be expected to dress in frock coats at formal ceremonies, or to attend public entertainments in swallow-tails? Public meetings were held to discuss the subject, and the new style of dress was condemned as unsuitable. At the same time it was thought by many that the present dresses of men and women leave much room for improvement. It should be mentioned that as soon as it was known that the dress uniform was under discussion in Parliament, the silk, hat and other trades guilds, imitating the habits of the wide-world which always everywhere considers self first, fearing that the contemplated change in dress might injuriously affect their respective interests, sent delegates to Peking to "lobby" the members to "go slow" and not to introduce too radical changes. The result was that in addition to the two forms of dress above mentioned, two more patterns were authorized, one for man's ordinary wear and the other for women, both following Chinese styles, but all to be made of home-manufactured material. This was to soothe the ruffled feelings of the manufacturers and traders, for in purchasing a foreign suit some of the materials at least, if not all, must be of foreign origin or foreign make.

During a recent visit to Peking I protested against this novel fashion, and submitted a memorandum to President Yuan with a request that it should be transmitted to Parliament. My suggestion is that the frock-coat and evening-dress regulation should be optional, and that the Chinese dress uniform as sketched by me in my memorandum should be adopted as an alternative. I am in hopes that my suggestion will be favorably considered. The point I have taken is that Chinese diplomats and others who go abroad should, in order to avoid curiosity, and for the sake of uniformity, adopt Western dress, and that those who are at home, if they prefer the ugly change, should be at liberty to adopt it, but that it should not be compulsory on others who object to suffering from cold in winter, or to being liable to sunstroke in summer. I have taken this middle course in order to satisfy both sides; for it would be difficult to induce Parliament to abolish or alter what has been so recently fixed by them. The Chinese dress, as is well known all over the world, is superior to that worn by civilized people in the West, and the recent change favored by the Chinese is deplored by most foreigners in China. The following paragraph, written by a foreign merchant and published in one of the Shanghai papers, expresses the opinion of almost all intelligent foreigners on this subject:

> Some time back the world was jubilant over the news that among the great reforms adopted in China was the discarding of the Chinese tunic, that great typical national costume. 'They are indeed getting civilized,' said the gossip; and one and all admired the energy displayed by the resolute Young China in coming into line with the CIVILIZED world, adopting even our uncomfortable, anti-hygienic and anti-esthetic costume.
>
> Foreign 'fashioned' tailor shops, hat stores, shoemakers, etc., sprang up all over the country. When I passed through Canton in September last, I could not help noticing also that those typical streets lined with boat-shaped, high-soled shoes, had been replaced by foreign-style boot and shoemakers.
>
> Undoubtedly the reform was gaining ground and the Chinese would have to be in the future depicted dressed up as a Caucasian.
>
> In my simplicity I sincerely confess I could not but deplore the passing away of the century-old tunic, so esthetic, so comfortable, so rich, so typical of the race. In my heart I was sorry for the change, as to my conception it was not in the dress where the Chinese had to seek reform. . . .

I agree with this writer that it is not in the domain of dress that we Chinese should learn from the Western peoples. There are many things in China which could be very well improved, but certainly not dress.

Notes

* *The Clothes Question Considered in its Relation to Beauty, Comfort and Health*, by Mrs. M. S. G. Nichols. Published in London, 32 Fopstone Road, Earl's Court, S.W.
** There have been a few cases of Chinese workmen who through carelessness have exposed themselves by working in the sun; but such cases are rare.

12

American versus Chinese Civilization (continued)

The question has often been asked "Which are the civilized nations?" And the answer has been, "All Europe and America." To the query, "What about the nations in the East?" the answer has been made that, with the exception of Japan, who has now become a great civilized power, the other nations are more or less civilized. When the matter is further pressed and it is asked, "What about China?" the general reply is, "She is semi-civilized," or in other words, not so civilized as the nations in the West.

Before pronouncing such an opinion justifiable, let us consider the plain facts. I take it that civilization inculcates culture, refinement, humane conduct, fair dealing and just treatment. Amiel says, "Civilization is first and foremost a moral thing." There is no doubt that the human race, especially in the West, has improved wonderfully within the last century. Many inventions and discoveries have been made, and men are now able to enjoy comforts which could not have been obtained before.

From a material point of view we have certainly progressed, but do the "civilized" people in the West live longer than the so-called semi-civilized races? Have they succeeded in prolonging their lives? Are they happier than others? I should like to hear their answers. Is it not a fact that Americans are more liable to catch cold than Asiatics; with the least change of air, and with the slightest appearance of an epidemic are they not more easily infected than Asiatics? If so, why? With their genius for invention why have they not discovered means to safeguard themselves so that they can live longer on this earth? Again, can Americans say that they are happier than the Chinese? From personal observation I have formed the opinion that the Chinese are more contented than Americans, and on the whole happier; and certainly one meets more old people in China than in America. Since the United States of America is rich, well governed, and provided with more material comforts than China, Americans, one would think, should be happier than we are, but are they? Are there not many in their midst who are friendless and penurious? In China no man is without friends, or if he is, it is his own fault. "Virtue is never friendless," said Confucius, and, as society is constituted in China, this is literally true. If this is not so in America I fear there is something wrong with that boasted civilization, and that their material triumphs over the physical forces of nature have been paid dearly for by a loss of insight into her profound spiritualities. Perhaps some will understand when I quote Lao Tsze's address to Confucius on "Simplicity":

> The chaff from winnowing will blind a man. Mosquitoes will bite a man and keep him awake all night, and so it is with all the talk of yours about charity and duty to one's neighbor, it drives one crazy. Sir, strive to keep the world in its original simplicity ~ why so much fuss? The wind blows as it listeth, so let virtue establish itself. The swan is white without a daily bath, and the raven is black without dyeing itself. When the pond is dry and the fishes are gasping for breath it is of no use to moisten them with a little water or a little sprinkling. Compared to their original and simple condition in the pond and the rivers it is nothing.

Henry Ward Beecher says, "Wealth may not produce civilization, but civilization produces money," and in my opinion while wealth may be used to promote happiness and health it as often injures both. Happiness is the product of liberality, intelligence and service to others, and the reflex of happiness is health. My contention is that the people who possess these good qualities in the greatest degree are the most civilized. Now civilization, as mentioned in the previous chapter, was born in the East and travelled westward. The law of nature is spiral, and inasmuch as Eastern civilization taught the people of the West, so Western civilization, which is based upon principles native to the East, will return to its original source. No nation can now remain shut up within itself without intercourse with other nations; the East and the West can no longer exist separate and apart. The new facilities for transportation and travel by land and water bring all nations, European, American, Asiatic, and African, next door to each other, and when the art of aviation is more advanced and people travel in the air as safely as they now cross oceans, the relationships of nations will become still closer.

What effect will this have on mankind? The first effect will be, I should say, greater stability. As interests become common, destructive combats will vanish. All alike will be interested in peace. It is a gratifying sign that within recent years the people of America have taken a prominent part in peace movements, and have inaugurated peace congresses, the members of which represent different sections of the country. Annual gatherings of this order must do much to prevent war and to perpetuate peace, by turning people's thoughts in the right direction. Take, for instance, the Lake Mohonk Conference on International Arbitration, which was started by a private gentleman, Mr. A. K. Smiley, who was wont every year to invite prominent officials and others to his beautiful summer place at Lake Mohonk for a conference. He has passed away, to the regret of his many friends, but the good movement still continues, and the nineteenth annual conference was held under the auspices of his brother, Mr. Daniel Smiley. Among those present, there were not only eminent Americans, such as Dr. C. W. Eliot, President Emeritus of Harvard University, Ex-American Ambassador C. Tower, Dr. J. Taylor, President of Vassar College, and Dr. Lyman Abbott, but distinguished foreigners such as J. A. Baker, M.P., of England, Herr Heinrich

York Steiner, of Vienna, and many others. Among the large number of people who support this kind of movement, and the number is increasing every day, the name of Mr. Andrew Carnegie stands out very prominently. This benevolent gentleman is a most vigorous advocate of International Peace, and has spent most of his time and money for that purpose. He has given ten million dollars in gold for the purpose of establishing the Carnegie Peace Fund; the first paragraph in his long letter to the trustees is worthy of reproduction, as it expresses his strong convictions:

> "I have transferred to you," he says, "as Trustees of the Carnegie Peace Fund, ten million dollars of five percent mortgage bonds, the revenue of which is to be administered by you to hasten the abolition of international war, the foulest blot upon our civilization. Although we no longer eat our fellowmen nor torture our prisoners, nor sack cities, killing their inhabitants, we still kill each other in war like barbarians. Only wild beasts are excusable for doing that in this the Twentieth Century of the Christian era, for the crime of war is inherent, since it decides not in favor of the right, but always of the strong. The nation is criminal which refuses arbitration and drives its adversary to a tribunal which knows nothing of righteous judgment."

I am glad to say that I am familiar with many American magazines and journals which are regularly published to advocate peace, and I have no doubt that in every country similar movements are stirring, for the nations are beginning to realize the disastrous effects of war. If I am not mistaken, however, Americans are the most active in this matter. The Permanent Court of Arbitration at The Hague, whose members belong to nearly every nation, is a significant index of the spirit of the times. Yet what an irony of fate that while people are so active in perpetuating peace they cannot preserve it. Look at the recent wars in Europe, first between Italy and Turkey, and afterward in the Balkans, to say nothing of disturbances in China and other parts of the world. It is just like warning a child not to take poison and then allowing him to swallow it and die. Sensible men should consider this question calmly and seriously. We all agree as to the wickedness of war and yet we war with one another; we do not like war yet we cannot help war. There is surely some hidden defect in the way we have been brought up.

Is not the slogan of nationality, to a great extent, the root of the evil? Every schoolboy and schoolgirl is taught the duty of devotion, or strong attachment, to his or her own country, and every statesman or public man preaches the doctrine of loyalty to one's native land; while the man who dares to render service to another country, the interests of which are opposed to the interests of his own land, is denounced a traitor. In such cases the individual is never allowed an opinion as to the right or wrong of the dispute. He is expected to support his own country and to cry at all times, "Our country, right or wrong." A politician's best chance to secure votes is to gloss over the faults of his own party or nation, to dilate on the wickedness of his neighbors and to exhort his compatriots to be loyal to their national flag. Can it be wondered at that men who are imbued with such doctrines become selfish and narrow-minded and are easily involved in quarrels with other nations?

Patriotism is, of course, the national life. Twenty-four centuries ago, speaking in the Greek colony of Naxos, Pythagoras described this emotion in the following eloquent passage: "Listen, my children, to what the State should be to the good citizen. It is more than father or mother, it is more than husband or wife, it is more than child or friend. The State is the father and mother of all, is the wife of the husband and the husband of the wife. The family is good, and good is the joy of the man in wife and in son. But greater is the State, which is the protector of all, without which the home would be ravaged and destroyed. Dear to the good man is the honor of the woman who bore him, dear the honor of the wife whose children cling to his knees; but dearer should be the honor of the State that keeps safe the wife and the child. It is the State from which comes all that makes your life prosperous, and gives you beauty and safety. Within the State are built up the arts, which make the difference between the barbarian and the man. If the brave man dies gladly for the hearthstone, far more gladly should he die for the State."

But only when the State seeks the good of the governed, for said Pythagoras on another occasion: "Organized society exists for the happiness and welfare of its members; and where it fails to secure these it stands *ipso facto* condemned."

101

But today, should the State be at war with another, and any citizen or section of citizens believe their own country wrong and the opposing nation wronged, they dare not say so, or if they do they run great risk of being punished for treason. Men and women, though no longer bought and sold in the market place, are subjected to subtler forms of serfdom. In most European countries they are obliged to fight whether they will or not, and irrespective of their private convictions about the dispute; even though, as is the case in some European countries, they may be citizens from compulsion rather than choice, they are not free to abstain from active participation in the quarrel. Chinese rebellions are said to "live on loot," i.e. on the forcible confiscation of private property, but is that worse than winning battles on the forcible deprivation of personal liberty? This is nationalism gone mad! It fosters the desire for territory grabbing and illustrates a fundamental difference between the Orient and the Occident. With us government is based on the consent of the governed in a way that the Westerner can hardly understand, for his passion to expand is chronic. Small nations which are over-populated want territory for their surplus population; great nations desire territory to extend their trade, and when there are several great powers to divide the spoil they distribute it among themselves and call it "spheres of influence," and all in honor of the god Commerce. In China the fundamentals of our social system are brotherhood and the dignity of labor.

What, I ask, is the advantage of adding to national territory? Let us examine the question calmly. If a town or a province is seized the conqueror has to keep a large army to maintain peace and order, and unless the people are well disposed to the new authority there will be constant trouble and friction. All this, I may say, in passing, is opposed to our Confucian code, which bases everything on reason and abhors violence. We would rather argue with a mob and find out, if possible, its point of view, than fire on it. We have yet to be convinced that good results flow from the use of the sword and the cannon. Western nations know no other compulsion.

If, however, the acquisition of new territory arises from a desire to develop the country and to introduce the most modern and improved systems of government, without ulterior intentions, then it is beyond praise, but I fear that such disinterested actions are rare. The nearest approach to such high principle is the purchase of the Philippine Islands by the United States. I call it "purchase" because the United States Government paid a good price for the islands after having seized the territory. The intentions of the Government were well known at the time. Since her acquisition of those islands, America has been doing her best to develop their resources and expand their trade. Administrative and judicial reforms have been introduced, liberal education has been given to the natives, who are being trained for self-government. It has been repeatedly and authoritatively declared by the United States that as soon as they are competent to govern themselves without danger of disturbances, and are able to establish a stable government, America will grant independence to those islands. I believe that when the proper time comes she will fulfill her word, and thus set a noble example to the world.

The British in Hong Kong afford an illustration of a different order, proving the truth of my contention that, excepting as a sphere for the exercise of altruism, the acquisition of new territories is an illusive gain. When Hong Kong was ceded to Great Britain at the conclusion of a war in which China was defeated, it was a bare island containing only a few fishermen's huts. In order to make it a trading port and encourage people to live there, the British Government spent large sums of money year after year for its improvement and development, and through the wise administration of the local Government every facility was afforded for free trade. It is now a prosperous British colony with a population of nearly half a million. But what have been the advantages to Great Britain? Financially she has been a great loser, for the island which she received at the close of her war with China was for many years a great drain on her national treasury. Now Hong Kong is a self-supporting colony, but what benefits do the British enjoy there that do not belong to everyone else? The colony is open to all foreigners, and every right which a British merchant has is equally shared with everyone else. According to the census of 1911, out of a population of 456,739 only 12,075 were non-Chinese, of whom a small portion were British; the rest were Chinese. Thus the prosperity of that colony depends upon the Chinese who, it is needless to say, are in possession of all the privileges that are enjoyed by British residents. It should be noticed that the number of foreign (i.e. non-British) firms and stores have been, and are, increasing, while big British *hongs*˙ are less numerous than before. Financially, the British people have certainly not been gainers by the acquisition of that colony. Of course I shall be told that it adds to the prestige of Great Britain, but this is an empty, bumptious boast dearly paid for by the British tax-payer.

From an economic and moral point of view, however, I must admit that a great deal of good has been done by the British Government in Hong Kong. It has provided the Chinese with an actual working model of a Western system of government which, notwithstanding many difficulties, has succeeded in transforming a barren island into a prosperous town, which is now the largest shipping port in China. The impartial administration of law and the humane treatment of criminals cannot but excite admiration and gain the confidence of the natives. If the British Government, in acquiring the desert island, had for its purpose the instruction of the natives in a modern system of government, she is to be sincerely congratulated, but it is feared that her motives were less altruistic.

These remarks apply equally, if not with greater force, to the other colonies or possessions in China under the control of European Powers, as well as to the other colonies of the British Empire, such as Australia, New Zealand, Canada, and others which are called "self-governing dominions". The Imperial Government feels very tender toward these colonists, and practically they are allowed to manage their affairs as they like. Since they are so generously treated and enjoy the protection of so great a power, there is no fear that these self-governing dominions will ever become independent of their mother country; but if they ever should do so, it is most improbable that she would declare war against them, as the British people have grown wiser since their experience with the American colonists. British statesmen have been awakened to the necessity of winning the good-will of their colonists, and within recent years have adopted the policy of inviting the Colonial premiers to London to discuss questions affecting Imperial and Colonial interests. Imperial federation seems to be growing popular with the British and it is probable that in the future England, Scotland, Wales, and Ireland will each have its own parliament, with an Imperial Parliament, sitting at Westminster, containing representatives from all parts of the British Empire, but America is the only nation which has added to her responsibilities with the avowed purpose of making semi-civilized tribes independent, self-governing colonies, and America is almost the only great power that has never occupied or held territory in China.

Let me ask again what is the object of nations seeking new possessions? Is it for the purpose of trade? If so, the object can be obtained without acquiring territory. In these days of enlightenment anyone can go to any country and trade without restriction, and in the British colonies the alien is in the same position as the native. He is not hampered by "permits" or other "red-tape" methods. Is it for the purpose of emigration? In Europe, America and all the British colonies, so far as I know, white people, unless they are paupers or undesirables, can emigrate to any country and after a short period become naturalized.

Some statesmen would say that it is necessary for a great power to have naval bases or coaling stations in several parts of the world. This presupposes preparations for war; but if international peace were maintained, such possessions would be useless and the money spent on them wasted. In any case it is unproductive expenditure. It is the fashion for politicians (and I am sorry to find them supported by eminent statesmen) to preach the doctrine of armaments; they allege that in order to preserve peace it is necessary to be prepared for war, that a nation with a large army or navy commands respect, and that her word carries weight. This argument cuts both ways, for a nation occupying such a commanding position may be unreasonable and a terror to weaker nations. If this high-toned doctrine continues where will it end? We shall soon see every nation arming to the teeth for the sake of her national honor and safety, and draining her treasury for the purpose of building dreadnaughts and providing armaments. When such a state of things exists can international peace be perpetuated? Will not occasion be found to test those war implements and to utilize the naval and military men? When you purchase a knife don't you expect to use it? Mr. Lloyd George, the English Chancellor of the Exchequer, in a speech in which he lamented the ever-increasing but unnecessary expenditure on armaments, said in Parliament: "I feel confident that it will end in a great disaster ~ I won't say to this country, though it is just possible that it may end in a disaster here." A man with a revolver sometimes invites attack, lest what was at first intended only for a defense should become a menace.

When discussing the craze of the Western nations for adding to their territories I said that white people can emigrate to any foreign country that they please, but it is not so with the yellow race. It has been asserted with authority that some countries are reserved exclusively for the white races, and with this object in view laws have been enacted prohibiting the natives of Asia from becoming naturalized citizens, besides imposing very strict and almost prohibitory regulations regarding their admission. Those who support such a policy hold that they, the white people, are superior to the yellow people in intellect, in education, in taste, and in habits, and that the yellow people are unworthy to associate with them. Yet in China we have manners, we have arts, we have morals, and we have managed a fairly large society for thousands of years without the bitter class hatreds, class divisions, and class struggles that have marred the fair progress of the West. We have not enslaved our lives to wealth. We like luxury, but we like other things better. We love life more than chasing imitations of life.

Our differences of color, like our differences of speech, are accidental, they are due to climatic and other influences. We came originally from one stock. We all started evenly, Heaven has no favorites. Man alone has made differences between man and man, and the yellow man is no whit inferior to the white people in intelligence. During the Russo-Japan War was it not the yellow race that displayed the superior intelligence? I am sometimes almost tempted to say that Asia will have to civilize the West over again. I am not bitter or sarcastic, but I do contend that there are yet many things that the white races have to learn from their colored brethren. In India, in China, and in Japan there are institutions which have a stability unknown outside Asia. Religion has apparently little influence on Western civilization; it is the corner-stone of society in all Asiatic civilizations. The result is that the colored races place morality in the place assigned by their more practical white confreres to economic propositions. We think, as we contemplate the West, that white people do not understand comfort because they have no leisure to enjoy contentment; THEY measure life by accumulation, WE by morality. Family ties are stronger with the so-called colored races than they are among the more irresponsible white races; consequently the social sense is keener among the former and much individual suffering is avoided. We have our vices, but these are not peculiar to US; and, at least, we have the merit of being easily governed. Wherever there are Chinese colonies the general verdict is: "The Chinese make good citizens."

This is what the late Sir Robert Hart, to whom China owes her Customs organization, said about us:

> They (the Chinese) are well-behaved, law-abiding, intelligent, economical, and industrious; they can learn anything and do anything; they are punctiliously polite, they worship talent, and they believe in right so firmly that they scorn to think it requires to be supported or enforced by might; they delight in literature, and everywhere they have their literary clubs and coteries for learning and discussing each other's essays and verses; they possess and practise an admirable system of ethics, and they are generous, charitable, and fond of good work; they never forget a favor, they make rich return for any kindness, and though they know money will buy service, a man must be more than wealthy to win esteem and respect; they are practical, teachable, and wonderfully gifted with common sense; they are excellent artisans, reliable workmen, and of a good faith that everyone acknowledges and admires in their commercial dealings; in no country that is or was, has the commandment 'Honor thy father and thy mother,' been so religiously obeyed, or so fully and without exception given effect to, and it is in fact the keynote of their family, social, official and national life, and because it is so their days are long in the land God has given them.

The cry of "America for the Americans" or "Australia for the Australians" is most illogical, for those people were not the original owners of the soil; with far greater reason we in the far East might shout, "China for the Chinese," "Japan for the Japanese." I will quote Mr. T. S. Sutton, English Secretary of the Chinese-American League of Justice, on this point. "The most asinine whine in the world," he says, "is that of 'America for the Americans' or 'China for the Chinese,' etc. It is the hissing slogan of greed, fear, envy, selfishness, ignorance and prejudice. No man, no human being who calls himself a man, no Christian, no sane or reasonable person, should or could ever be guilty of uttering that despicable wail. God made the world for all men, and if God has any preference, if God is any respecter of persons, He must surely favor the Chinese, for He has made more of them than of any other people on the globe. 'America for the aboriginal Indians' was once the cry. Then when the English came over it changed to 'America for the English,' later 'America for the Puritans,' and around New Orleans they cried 'America for the French.' In Pennsylvania the slogan was 'America for the Dutch,' etc., but the truth remains that God has set aside America as 'the melting pot' of the world, the land to which all people may come, and from which there has arisen, and will continue to rise, a great mixed race, a cosmopolitan nation that may, if it is not misled by prejudice and ignorance, yet lead the world." Although Mr. Sutton's phraseology is somewhat strong, his arguments are sound and unanswerable.

I now pass to some less controversial aspects of my theme, and note a praiseworthy custom that is practically unknown in the Far East. I refer to the habit of international marriages which are not only common in cosmopolitan America, but are of daily occurrence in Europe also, among ordinary people as well as the royal families of Europe, so that nearly all the European courts are related one to the other. This is a good omen for a permanent world-peace. There have been some marriages of Asiatics with Europeans and Americans, and they should be encouraged. Everything that brings the East and West together and helps each to understand the other better, is good. The offspring from such mixed unions inherit the good points of both sides. The head master of the Queen's College in Hong Kong, where there are hundreds of boys of different nationalities studying together, once told me that formerly at the yearly examination the prizes were nearly all won by the Chinese students, but that in later years when Eurasian boys were admitted, they beat the Chinese and all the others, and generally came out the best. Not only in school, but in business also they have turned out well. It is well known that the richest man in Hong Kong is a Eurasian. It is said that the father of Aguinaldo, the well-known Philippine leader, was a Chinese. There is no doubt that mixed marriages of the white with the yellow races will be productive of good to both sides. But do Chinese really make good husbands? my lady friends ask. I will cite the case of an American lady. Some years ago a

Chinese called on me at my Legation in Washington accompanied by an American lady and a girl. The lady was introduced to me as his wife and the girl as his daughter; I naturally supposed that the lady was the girl's mother, but she told me that the girl was the daughter of her late intimate friend, and that after her death, knowing that the child's father had been a good and affectionate husband to her friend, she had gladly become his second wife, and adopted his daughter.

Those who believe in reincarnation (and I hope most of my readers do, as it is a clue to many mysteries) understand that when people are reincarnated they are not always born in the same country or continent as that in which they lived in their previous life. I have an impression that in one of my former existences I was born and brought up in the United States. In saying this I do not express the slightest regrets at having now been born in Asia. I only wish to give a hint to those white people who advocate an exclusive policy that in their next life they may be born in Asia or Africa, and that the injury they are now inflicting on the yellow people they may themselves have to suffer in another life.

While admitting that we Chinese have our faults and that in some matters we have much to learn, especially from the Americans, we at least possess one moral quality, magnanimity, while the primal virtues of industry, economy, obedience, and love of peace, combined with a "moderation in all things", are also common among us. Our people have frequently been slighted or ill-treated but we entertain no revengeful spirit, and are willing to forget. We believe that in the end right will conquer might. Innumerable as have been the disputes between Chinese and foreigners it can at least be said, without going into details, that we have not, in the first instance, been the aggressors. Let me supply a local illustration showing how our faults are always exaggerated. Western people are fond of horse-racing. In Shanghai they have secured from the Chinese a large piece of ground, where they hold race meetings twice a year, but no Chinese are allowed on the grand-stand during the race days. They are provided with a separate entrance, and a separate enclosure, as though they were the victims of some infectious disease. I have been told that a few years ago a Chinese gentleman took some Chinese ladies into the grand-stand and that they misbehaved; hence this discriminatory treatment of Chinese. It is proper that steps should be taken to preserve order and decency in public places, but is it fair to interdict the people of a nation on account of the misconduct of two or three? Suppose it had been Germans who had misbehaved themselves (which is not likely), would the race club have dared to exclude Germans from sharing with other nations the pleasures of the races?

In contrast with this, let us see what the Chinese have done. Having learned the game of horse-racing from the foreigners in China, and not being allowed to participate, they have formed their own race club, and, with intention, have called it the "International Recreation Club." This Club has purchased a large tract of land at Kiangwan, about five miles from Shanghai, and has turned it into a race-course, considerably larger than that in Shanghai. When a race meeting is held there, IT IS OPEN TO FOREIGNERS AS WELL AS CHINESE, in fact complimentary tickets have even been sent to the members of the foreign race club inviting their attendance. Half of the members of the race committee are foreigners; while foreigners and Chinese act jointly as stewards and judges; the ponies that run are owned by foreigners as well as by Chinese, and Chinese jockeys compete with foreign jockeys in all the events. A most pleasing feature of these races is the very manifest cordial good feeling which prevails throughout the races there. The Chinese have been dubbed "semi-civilized and heathenish," but the "International Recreation Club" and the Kiangwan racecourse display an absence of any desire to retaliate and sentiments of international friendship such as it would, perhaps, be difficult to parallel. Should such people be denied admission into Australia, Canada, or the United States? Would not the exclusionists in those countries profit by association with them?

The immigration laws in force in Australia are, I am informed, even more strict and more severe than those in the United States. They amount to almost total prohibition; for they are directed not only against Chinese laborers but are so operated that the Chinese merchant and student are also practically refused admission. In the course of a lecture delivered in England by Mrs. Annie Besant in 1912 on "The citizenship of colored races in the British Empire," while condemning the race prejudices of her own people, she brought out a fact which will be interesting to my readers, especially to the

Australians. She says, "In Australia a very curious change is taking place. Color has very much deepened in that clime, and the Australian has become very yellow; so that it becomes a problem whether, after a time, the people would be allowed to live in their own country. The white people are far more colored than are some Indians." In the face of this plain fact is it not time, for their own sake, that the Australians should drop their cry against yellow people and induce their Parliament to abolish, or at least to modify, their immigration laws with regard to the yellow race? Australians are anxious to extend their trade, and they have sent commercial commissioners to Japan and other Eastern countries with the view to developing and expanding commerce. Mr. J. B. Suttor, Special Commissioner of New South Wales, has published the following advertisement:

NEW SOUTH WALES. The Land of Reward for Capital Commerce and Industry. Specially subsidized steamers now giving direct service between Sydney, THE PREMIER COMMERCIAL CENTER OF AUSTRALIA, AND SHANGHAI. Thus offering special facilities for Commerce and Tourists. NEW SOUTH WALES PRODUCTS ARE STANDARDS OF EXCELLENCE.

Commerce and friendship go together, but how Australians can expect to develop trade in a country whose people are not allowed to come to visit her shores even for the purposes of trade, passes my comprehension. Perhaps, having heard so much of the forgiving and magnanimous spirit of the Chinese, Australians expect the Chinese to greet them with smiles and to trade with them, while being kicked in return.

I believe in the doctrine of the universal brotherhood of men. It is contrary to the law of creation that some people should shut out other people from portions of the earth solely from motives of selfishness and jealousy; the injury caused by such selfish acts will sooner or later react on the doers. 'Every man is his own ancestor. We are preparing for the days that come, and we are what we are today on account of what has gone before." The dog-in-the-manger policy develops doggish instincts in those who practise it; and, after all, civilization without kindness and justice is not worth having. In conclusion, I will let the English poet, William Wordsworth, state "Nature's case."

Listen to these noble lines from the ninth canto of his "Excursion":

Alas! what differs more than man from man,
And whence that difference? Whence but from himself?
For see the universal Race endowed
With the same upright form. The sun is fixed
And the infinite magnificence of heaven
Fixed, within reach of every human eye;
The sleepless ocean murmurs for all years;
The vernal field infuses fresh delight
Into all hearts. Throughout the world of sense,
Even as an object is sublime or fair,
That object is laid open to the view
Without reserve or veil; and as a power
Is salutary, or an influence sweet,
Are each and all enabled to perceive
That power, that influence, by impartial law,
Gifts nobler are vouchsafed alike to all;
Reason, and, with that reason, smiles and tears;
Imagination, freedom in the will;
Conscience to guide and check; and death to be
Foretasted, immortality conceived
By all - a blissful immortality,
To them whose holiness on earth shall make
The Spirit capable of heaven, assured.

...The smoke ascends
To Heaven as lightly from the cottage hearth
As from the haughtiest palace. He whose soul
Ponders this true equality, may walk
The fields of earth with gratitude and hope;
Yet, in that meditation, will he find

Motive to sadder grief, as we have found;
Lamenting ancient virtues overthrown,
And for the injustice grieving, that hath made
So wide a difference between man and man.

Notes

* Cantonese for 'trading company.'

13

Dinners, Banquets, etc.

Dinner, as we all know, indicates a certain hour and a certain habit whose aim is the nourishment of the body, and a deliverance from hunger; but in our modern civilized life it possesses other purposes also. Man is a gregarious animal, and when he takes his food he likes company; from this peculiarity there has sprung up the custom of dinner parties. In attending dinner parties, however, the guests as a rule do not seek sustenance, they only go to them when they have nothing else to do, and many scarcely touch the food that is laid before them. Their object is to do honor to the host and hostess, not to eat, but to be entertained by pleasant and congenial conversation. Nevertheless, the host, at whose invitation the company has assembled, is expected to provide a great abundance and a large variety of savory dishes, as well as a good supply of choice wines. Flesh and wine are indispensable, even though the entertainers eschew both in their private life, and most of the guests daily consume too much of each. Few have the courage to part with conventional practices when arranging a social function.

American chefs are excellent caterers, and well know how to please the tastes of the American people. They concentrate on the art of providing dainty dishes, and human ingenuity is heavily taxed by them in their efforts to invent new gustatory delicacies. The dishes which they place before each guest are so numerous that even a gourmand must leave some untouched. At a fashionable dinner no one can possibly taste, much less eat, everything that is placed before him, yet the food is all so nicely cooked, and served in so appetizing a manner, that it is difficult to resist the temptation at least to sample it; when you have done this, however, you will continue eating until all has been finished, but your stomach will probably be a sad sufferer, groaning grievously on the following day on account of the frolic of your palate. This ill-mated pair, although both are chiefly interested in food, seldom seem to agree. I must not omit to mention however that the number of courses served at an American millionaire's dinner is after all less numerous than those furnished at a Chinese feast. When a Chinese gentleman asks his friends to dine with him the menu may include anywhere from thirty to fifty or a hundred courses; but many of the dishes are only intended for show. The guests are not expected to eat everything on the table, or even to taste every delicacy, unless, indeed, they specially desire to do so. Again, we don't eat so heartily as do the Americans, but content ourselves with one or two mouthfuls from each set of dishes, and allow appreciable intervals to elapse between courses, during which we make merry, smoke, and otherwise enjoy the company. This is a distinct advantage in favor of China.

In Europe and America, dessert forms the last course at dinner; in China this is served first. I do not know which is the better way. Chinese are ever ready to accept the best from every quarter, and so many of us have recently adopted the Western practice regarding dessert, while still retaining the ancient Chinese custom, so that now we eat sweetmeats and fruit at the beginning, during dinner, and at the end. This happy combination of Eastern and Western practices is, I submit, worthy of expansion and extension. If it were to become universal it would help to discourage the present unwholesome habit, for it is nothing more than a habit, of devouring flesh.

One of the dishes indispensable at a fashionable American dinner is the terrapin. Those who eat these things say that their flesh has a most agreeable and delicate flavor, and that their gelatinous skinny necks and fins are delicious, but apparently the most palatable tidbits pall the taste in time, for it is said that about forty years ago terrapins were so abundant and cheap that workmen in their agreement with their employers stipulated that terrapin should not be supplied at their dinner table more than three times a week. Since then terrapins have become so rare that no stylish dinner ever takes place without this dish. Oysters are another Western *sine qua non*, and are always served raw. I wonder how many ladies and gentlemen who swallow these mollusca with such evident relish know that they are veritable scavengers, which pick up and swallow every dirty thing in the water. A friend of mine after taking a few of them on one occasion had to leave the table and go home; he was ill afterward for several days. One cannot be too careful as to what one eats. The United States has a Pure Food Department, but I think it might learn a great deal that it does not know if it were to send a commission to China to study life in the Buddhist monasteries, where only sanitary, healthful food is consumed. It is always a surprise to me that people are so indifferent to the kind of food they take. Public health officers are useful officials, but when we have become more civilized each individual will be his own health officer.

Some of the well-known Chinese dishes are very relishable and should not be overlooked by chefs and dinner hostesses. I refer to the sharks' fins, and birds' nest - the Eastern counterpart of the Western *piece de resistance* - the terrapin. From a hygienic point of view, sharks' fins may not be considered as very desirable, seeing they are part of the shark, but they are certainly not worse, and are perhaps better, than what is called the "high and tender" pheasant, and other flesh foods which are constantly found on Western dining tables, and which are so readily eaten by connoisseurs. Birds' nest soup is far superior to turtle soup, and I have the opinion of an American chemist who analyzed it, that it is innocuous and minus the injurious uric acid generated by animal flesh, the cause of rheumatic and similar painful complaints.

The "*chop suey*" supplied in the Chinese restaurants in New York, Chicago, and other places, seems to be a favorite dish with the American public. It shows the similarity of our tastes, and encourages me to expect that some of my recommendations will be accepted.

Will some one inform me why so many varieties of wines are always served on American tables, and why the sparkling champagne is never avoidable? Wealthy families will spare neither pains nor expense to spread most sumptuous dinners, and it has been reported that the cost of an entertainment given by one rich lady amounted to twenty thousand pounds sterling, although, as I have said, eating is the last thing for which the guests assemble.

I do not suppose that many will agree with me, but in my opinion it would be much more agreeable, and improve the general conversation, if all drinks of an intoxicating nature were abolished from the dining table. It is gratifying to know that there are some families (may the number increase every day!) where intoxicating liquors are never seen on their tables. The first instance of this sort that came under my notice was in the home of that excellent woman, Mrs. M. F. Henderson, who is an ardent advocate of diet reform and teetotalism. Mr. William Jennings Bryan, the Secretary of State, has set a noble example, as from newspaper reports it appears that he gave a farewell dinner to Ambassador Bryce, without champagne or other alcoholic drinks. He has a loyal supporter in Shanghai, in the person of the American Consul-General, Dr. A. P. Wilder, who, to the great regret of everybody who knows him in this port, is retiring from the service on account of ill-health. Dr. Wilder is very popular and figures largely in the social life of the community, but Dr. Wilder is a staunch opponent of alcohol, and through his influence wines at public dinners are always treated as extras. So long as the liquor traffic is so extensively and profitably carried on in Europe and America, and so long as the consumption of alcohol is so enormous, so long will there be a difference of opinion as to its ill effects, but in this matter, by means of its State Prohibition Laws, America is setting an example to the world. In no other country are there such extensive tracts without alcohol as the "Dry States" of America. China, who is waging war on opium, recognizes in this fact a kindred, active moral force which is absent elsewhere, and, shaking hands with her sister republic across the seas, hopes that she will some day be as free of alcoholic poisons as China herself hopes to be of opium. Every vice, however, has its defense. Some years ago I met a famous Dutch artist in Peking, who, though still in the prime of life, was obliged to lay aside his work for a few days each month, due to an occasional attack of rheumatism. I found he was fond of his cup, though I did not understand that he was an immoderate drinker. I discoursed to him somewhat lengthily about the evil effects of drink, and showed him that unless he was willing to give up all intoxicating liquor, his rheumatism would never give him up. He listened attentively, pondered for a few minutes, and then gave this characteristic answer: "I admit the soundness of your argument but I enjoy my glass exceedingly; if I were to follow your advice I should be deprived of a lot of pleasure. Indeed, I would rather have the rheumatic pains, which disappear after two or three days, and continue to enjoy my alcoholic drinks, than endure the misery of doing without them." I warned him that in course of time his rheumatism would be longer in duration and attack him more frequently, if he continued to ignore its warnings and to play with what, for him, was certainly poison. When anyone has a habit, be it injurious or otherwise, it is not easy to persuade him to abandon it.

The Aristocracy of Health, written by the talented Mrs. Henderson, is an admirable work. I owe much to it. The facts and arguments adduced against tobacco smoking, strong drink and poisonous foods, are set forth in such a clear and convincing manner, that soon after reading it I became a teetotaler and "sanitarian"* and began at once to reap the benefits. I felt that I ought not to keep such a good thing to myself, but that I should preach the doctrine far and wide. I soon found, however, that it was an impossible task to try to save men from themselves, and I acquired the unenviable sobriquet of "crank"; but I was not dismayed. From my native friends I turned to the foreign community in Peking, thinking that the latter would possess better judgment, appreciate and be converted to the sanitarian doctrine. Among the foreigners I appealed to, one was a distinguished diplomat, and the other a gentleman in the Chinese service, with a world-wide reputation. Both were elderly and in delicate health, and it was my earnest hope that by reading Mrs. Henderson's book, which was sent to them, they would be convinced of their errors and turn over a new leaf - I was disappointed. Both, in returning the book, made substantially the same answer. "Mrs. Henderson's work is very interesting, but at my time of life it is not advisable to change life-long habits. I eat flesh moderately, and never drink much wine." They both seemed to overlook the crucial problem as to whether or not animal food contains hurtful poison. If it does, it should not be eaten at all. We never hear of sensible people taking arsenic, strychnine, or other poisons, in moderation, but many foolish women, I believe, take arsenic to pale their complexions, while others, both men and women, take strychnine in combination with other drugs, as a tonic, but will anyone argue that these substances are foods? The rule of moderation is applicable to things which are nutritious, or at least harmless, but not to noxious foods, however small the quantity of poison they may contain.

Pleasant conversation at the dinner table is always enjoyable, and a good talker is always welcome, but I often wonder why Americans, who generally are so quick to improve opportunity, and are noted for their freedom from traditional conventionalisms, do not make a more systematic use of the general love of good conversation. Anyone who is a witty conversationalist, with a large fund of anecdote, is sure to be asked by every dinner host to help to entertain the guests, but if the company be large the favorite can be enjoyed by only a few, and those who are too far away to hear, or who are just near enough to hear a part but not all, are likely to feel aggrieved. They cannot hear what is amusing the rest, while the talk elsewhere prevents their talking as they would if there were no interruptions. A raconteur generally monopolizes half the company, and leaves the other half out in the cold. This might be avoided if talkers were engaged to entertain the whole company during dinner, as pianists are now sometimes engaged to play to them after dinner. Or, the entertainment might be varied by engaging a good professional reciter to reproduce literary gems, comic or otherwise. I am sure the result would bring more general satisfaction to the guests than the present method of leaving them to entertain themselves. The Chinese employ singing girls; the Japanese, geishas to talk, sing or dance. The ideal would here again seem to be an amalgamation of East and West.

It is difficult for a mixed crowd to be always agreeable, even in the congenial atmosphere of a good feast, unless the guests have been selected with a view to their opinions rather than to their social standing. Place a number of people whose ideas are common, with a difference, around a well-spread table and there will be no lack of good, earnest, instructive conversation. Most men and women can talk well if they have the right sort of listeners. If the hearer is unsympathetic the best talker becomes dumb. Hosts who remember this will always be appreciated.

As a rule, a dinner conversation is seldom worth remembering, which is a pity. Man, the most sensible of all animals, can talk nonsense better than all the rest of his tribe. Perhaps the flow of words may be as steady as the eastward flow of the Yang-tse-Kiang in my own country, but the memory only retains a recollection of a vague, undefined - what? The conversation, like the flavors provided by the cooks, has been evanescent. Why should not hostesses make as much effort to stimulate the minds of their guests as they do to gratify their palates? What a boon it would be to many a bashful man, sitting next to a lady with whom he has nothing in common, if some public entertainer during the dinner relieved him from the necessity of always thinking of what he should say next? How much more he could enjoy the tasty dishes his hostess had provided; and as for the lady - what a number of suppressed yawns she might have avoided. To take great pains and spend large sums to provide nice food for people who cannot enjoy it because they have to talk to one another, seems a pity. Let one man talk to the rest and leave them leisure to eat, is my suggestion.

The opportunities afforded at the dining table may be turned to many useful purposes. Of course not all are ill-paired, and many young men and ladies meet, sit side by side, engage in a friendly, pleasant conversation, renew their acquaintance at other times, and finally merge their separate paths in the highway of marriage. Perhaps China might borrow a leaf from this custom and substitute dinner parties for go-betweens. The dinner-party method, however, has its dangers as well as its advantages - it depends on the point of view. Personal peculiarities and defects, if any, can be easily detected by the way in which the conversation is carried on, and the manner in which the food is handled. It has sometimes happened that the affianced have cancelled

121

their engagement after a dinner party. On the other hand, matters of great import can often be arranged at the dinner table better than anywhere else. Commercial transactions involving millions of dollars have frequently been settled while the parties were sipping champagne; even international problems, ending in elaborate negotiations and treaties, have been first discussed with the after-dinner cigar. The atmosphere of good friendship and equality, engendered by a well-furnished room, good cheer, pleasant company, and a genial hostess, disarms prejudice, removes barriers, melts reserve, and disposes one to see that there is another side to every question.

In China, when people have quarreled their friends generally invite them to dinner, where the matters in dispute are amicably arranged. These are called "peace dinners." I would recommend that a similar expedient should be adopted in America; many a knotty point could be disposed of by a friendly discussion at the dinner table. If international disputes were always arranged in this way the representatives of nations having complaints against each other might more often than now discover unexpected ways of adjusting their differences. Why should such matters invariably be remanded to formal conferences and set speeches? The preliminaries, at least, would probably be better arranged at dinner parties and social functions. Eating has always been associated with friendship. "To eat salt" with an Arab forms a most binding contract. Even "the serpent" in the book of Genesis commenced his acquaintance with Eve by suggesting a meal.

It almost seems as if there were certain unwritten laws in American society, assigning certain functions to certain days in the week. I do not believe Americans are superstitious, but I found that Thursday was greatly in favor. I remember on one occasion that Mrs. Grant, widow of the late President, sent an invitation to my wife and myself to dine at her house some Thursday evening; this was three weeks in advance, and we readily accepted her invitation. After our acceptance, about a dozen invitations came for that same Thursday, all of which we had, of course, to decline. Curiously enough we received no invitations for any other day during that week, and just before that eventful Thursday we received a letter from Mrs. Grant cancelling the invitation on account of the death of one of her relations, so that we had to dine at home after all. Now we Chinese make no such distinctions between days. Every day of the week is equally good; in order however to avoid clashing with other peoples' engagements, we generally fix Fridays for our receptions or dinners, but there is not among the Chinese an entertainment season as there is in Washington, and other great cities, when everybody in good society is busy attending or giving "At Homes," tea parties or dinners. I frequently attended "At Homes" or tea parties in half-a-dozen places or more in one afternoon, but no one can dine during the same evening in more than one place. In this respect America might learn a lesson from China. We can accept half-a-dozen invitations to dinner for one evening; all we have to do is to go to each place in turn, partake of one or two dishes, excuse ourselves to the host and then go somewhere else. By this means we avoid the seeming rudeness of a declination, and escape the ill feelings which are frequently created in the West by invitations being refused. The Chinese method makes possible the cultivation of democratic friendships without violating aristocratic instincts, and for candidates at election times it would prove an agreeable method by which to make new friends. We are less rigid than Americans about dropping in and taking a mouthful or two at dinner, even without a special invitation.*

Washington officials and diplomats usually give large entertainments. The arranging of the seats at the dinner table is a delicate matter, as the rule of precedence has to be observed, and inattention to the rule, by placing a wrong seat for a gentleman or lady who is entitled to a higher place, may be considered as a slight. It is at such functions as these that the professional story-teller, the good reciter, the clever reader, the perfect entertainer would make the natural selfish reserve of mankind less apparent.

Fashionable people who entertain a good deal are, I understand, often puzzled to know how to provide novelties. In addition to the suggestions I have made, may I be pardoned another? There are many good cooks in the U.S.A. Why not commission these to sometimes prepare a *recherche* Chinese dinner, with the food served in bowls instead of plates, and with chop-sticks ("nimble lads," we call them) for show, but forks and spoons for use. I see no reason why Chinese meals should not become fashionable in America, as Western preparations are frequently favored by the elite in China. One marked difference between the two styles is the manner in which the Chinese purveyor throws his most delicate flavors into strong relief by prefacing it with a diet which is insipid, harsh or pungent. Contrasts add zest to everything human, be it dining, working, playing, or wooing.

This suggests an occasional, toothsome vegetarian repast as a set-off to the same round of fish, flesh, fowl and wine fumes. No people in the world can prepare such delicious vegetarian banquets as a Chinese culinary artist.

A banquet is a more formal affair than the dinner parties I have been discussing. It is generally gotten up to celebrate some special event, such as the conclusion of some important business, or the birthday of some national hero like Washington, Lincoln, or Grant; or the Chambers of Commerce and Associations of different trades in the important cities of America will hold their annual meetings to hear a report and discuss the businesses transacted during the year, winding up by holding a large banquet.

The food supplied on these occasions is by no means superior to that given at private dinners, yet everybody is glad to be invited. It is the inevitable rule that speeches follow the eating, and people attend, not for the sake of the food, but for the privilege of hearing others talk. Indeed, except for the opportunity of talking, or hearing others talk, people would probably prefer a quiet meal at home. Speakers with a reputation, orators, statesmen, or foreign diplomats are frequently invited, and sometimes eminent men from other countries are the guests of honor. These functions occur every year, and the Foreign Ministers with whose countries the Associations have commercial relations are generally present.

The topics discussed are nearly always the same, and it is not easy to speak at one of these gatherings without going over the same ground as that covered on previous occasions. I remember that a colleague of mine who was a clever diplomat, and for whom I had great respect, once when asked to make an after-dinner speech, reluctantly rose and, as far as I can remember, spoke to the following effect: "Mr. Chairman and gentlemen, I thank your Association for inviting me to this splendid banquet, but as I had the honor of speaking at your banquet last year I have nothing more to add, and I refer you to that speech;" he then sat down. The novelty of his remarks, of course, won him applause, but I should like to know what the company really thought of him. For my part, I praised his wisdom, for he diplomatically rebuked all whose only interest is that which has its birth with the day and disappears with the night.

Banquets and dinners in America, as in China, are, however, often far removed from frivolities. Statesmen sometimes select these opportunities for a pronouncement of their policy, even the President of the nation may occasionally think it advisable to do this. Speeches delivered on such occasions are generally reported in all the newspapers, and, of course, discussed by all sorts of people, the wise and the otherwise, so that the speaker has to be very careful as to what he says. Our President confines himself to the more formal procedure of issuing an official mandate, the same in kind, though differing in expression, as an American President's Inaugural Address, or one of his Messages to Congress.

Commercial men do not understand and are impatient with the restrictions which hedge round a Foreign Minister, and in their anxiety to get speakers they will look anywhere. On one occasion I received an invitation to go to Canada to attend a banquet at a Commercial Club in one of the principal Canadian cities. It would have given me great pleasure to be able to comply with this request, as I had not then visited that country, but, contrary to inclination, I had to decline. I was accredited as Minister to Washington, and did not feel at liberty to visit another country without the special permission of my home Government.

Public speaking, like any other art, has to be cultivated. However scholarly a man may be, and however clever he may be in private conversation, when called upon to speak in public he may sometimes make a very poor impression. I have known highly placed foreign officials, with deserved reputations for wisdom and ability, who were shockingly poor speakers at banquets. They would hesitate and almost stammer, and would prove quite incapable of expressing their thoughts in any sensible or intelligent manner. In this respect, personal observations have convinced me that Americans, as a rule, are better speakers than. . . . (I will not mention the nationality in my mind, it might give offense.) An American, who, without previous notice, is called upon to speak, generally acquits himself creditably. He is nearly always witty, appreciative, and frank. This is due, I believe, to the thorough-going nature of his education: he is taught to be self-confident, to believe in his own ability to create, to express his opinions without fear. A diffident and retiring man, whose chief characteristic is extreme modesty, is not likely to be a good speaker; but Americans are free from this weakness. Far be it from me to suggest that there are no good speakers in other countries. America can by no means claim a monopoly of orators; there are many elsewhere whose sage sayings and forcible logic are appreciated by all who hear or read them; but, on the whole, Americans excel others in the readiness of their wit, and their power to make a good *extempore* speech on any subject, without opportunity for preparation.

Neither is the fair sex in America behind the men in this matter. I have heard some most excellent speeches by women, speeches which would do credit to an orator; but they labor under a disadvantage. The female voice is soft and low, it is not easily heard in a large room, and consequently the audience sometimes does not appreciate lady speakers to the extent that they deserve. However, I know a lady who possesses a powerful, masculine voice, and who is a very popular speaker, but she is an exception. Anyhow I believe the worst speaker, male or female, could improve by practising private declamation, and awakening to the importance of articulation, modulation, and - the pause.

Another class of social functions are "At Homes," tea parties and receptions. The number of guests invited to these is almost unlimited, it may be one or two dozen, or one or two dozen hundreds. The purpose of these is usually to meet some distinguished stranger, some guest in the house, or the newly married daughter of the hostess. It is impossible for the host or hostess to remember all those who attend, or even all who have been invited to attend; generally visitors leave their cards, although many do not even observe this rule, but walk right in as if they owned the house. When a newcomer is introduced his name is scarcely audible, and before the hostess, or the distinguished guest, has exchanged more than one or two words with him, another stranger comes along, so that it is quite excusable if the next time the hosts meet these people they do not recognize them. In China a new fashion is now in vogue; new acquaintances exchange cards. If this custom should be adopted in America there would be less complaints about new friends receiving the cold shoulder from those who they thought should have known them.

In large receptions, such as those mentioned above, however spacious the reception hall, in a great many instances there is not even standing room for all who attend. It requires but little imagination to understand the condition of the atmosphere when there is no proper ventilation. Now, what always astonished me was, that although the parlor might be crowded with ladies and gentlemen, all the windows were, as a rule, kept closed, with the result that the place was full of vitiated air. Frequently after a short time I have had to slip away when I would willingly have remained longer to enjoy the charming company. If I had done so, however, I should have taken into my lungs a large amount of the obnoxious atmosphere exhaled from hundreds of other persons in the room, to the injury of my health, and no one can give his fellows his best unless his health is hearty. No wonder we often hear of a host or hostess being unwell after a big function. Their feelings on the morning after are often the reverse of "good-will to men," and the cause is not a lowered moral heartiness but a weakened physical body through breathing too much air exhaled from other people's lungs. When man understands, he will make "good health" a religious duty.

In connection with this I quote Dr. J. H. Kellogg, the eminent physician and Superintendent of the Battle Creek Sanitarium. In his book, *The Living Temple* *, the doctor speaks as follows on the importance of breathing pure air: "The purpose of breathing is to obtain from the air a supply of oxygen, which the blood takes up and carries to the tissues. Oxygen is one of the most essential of all the materials required for the support of life. . . . The amount of oxygen necessarily required for this purpose is about one and one-fourth cubic inches for each breath. . . . In place of the one and one-fourth cubic inches of oxygen taken into the blood, a cubic inch of carbonic acid gas is given off, and along with it are thrown off various other still more poisonous substances which find a natural exit through the lungs. The amount of these combined poisons thrown off with a single breath is sufficient to contaminate, and render unfit to breathe, three cubic feet, or three-fourths of a barrel, of air. Counting an average of twenty breaths a minute for children and adults, the amount of air contaminated per minute would be three times twenty or sixty cubic feet, or one cubic foot a second. . . . Every one should become intelligent in relation to the matter of ventilation, and should appreciate its importance. Vast and irreparable injury frequently results from the confinement of several scores or hundreds of people in a schoolroom, church, or lecture room, without adequate means of removing the impurities thrown off from their lungs and bodies. The same air being breathed over and over becomes densely charged with poisons, which render the blood impure, lessen the bodily resistance, and induce susceptibility to taking cold, and to infection with the germs of pneumonia, consumption, and other infectious diseases, which are always present in a very crowded audience room. Suppose, for example, a thousand persons are seated in a room forty feet in width, sixty in length, and fifteen in height: how long a time would elapse before the air of such a room would become unfit for further respiration? Remembering that each person spoils one foot of air every second, it is clear that one thousand cubic feet of air will be contaminated for every second that the room is occupied. To ascertain the number of seconds which would elapse before the entire air contained in the room will be contaminated, so that it is unfit for further breathing, we have only to divide the cubic contents of the room by one thousand. Multiplying, we have 60*40*15 equals 36,000, the number of cubic feet. This, divided by one thousand, gives thirty-six as the number of seconds. Thus it appears that with closed doors and windows, breath poisoning of the audience would begin at the end of thirty-six seconds, or less than one minute. The condition of the air in such a room at the end of an hour cannot be adequately pictured in words, and yet hundreds of audiences are daily subjected to just such inhumane treatment through ignorance."

The above remarks apply not only to churches, lecture rooms, and other public places, but also with equal force to offices and family houses. I should like to know how many persons pay even a little attention to this important subject of pure air breathing? You go to an office, whether large or small, and you find all the windows closed, although there are half-a-dozen or more persons working in the room. No wonder that managers, clerks, and other office workers often break down and require a holiday to recuperate their impaired health at the seaside, or elsewhere.

When you call at a private residence you will find the same thing, all the windows closed. It is true that there are not so many persons in the room as in an office, but if your sense of smell is keen you will notice that the air has close, stuffy exhalations, which surely cannot be sanitary. If you venture to suggest that one of the windows be opened the lady of the house will at once tell you that you will be in a draught and catch cold.

It is a matter of daily occurrence to find a number of persons dining in a room where there is no opening for the contaminated air to leak out, or for the fresh air to come in. After dinner the gentlemen adjourn to the library to enjoy the sweet perfumes of smoking for an hour or so with closed windows. What a picture would be presented if the bacteria in the air could be sketched, enlarged, and thrown on a screen, or better still shown in a cinematograph, but apparently gentlemen do not mind anything so long as they can inhale the pernicious tobacco fumes.

It is a common practice, I fear, to keep the windows of the bedroom closed, except in hot weather. I have often suggested to friends that, for the sake of their health, they should at least keep one of the windows, if not more, open during the night, but they have pooh-poohed the idea on account of that bugaboo - a draught. It is one of the mysteries of the age that people should be willing to breathe second-hand air when there is so much pure, fresh air out of doors to be had for nothing; after inhaling and exhaling the same air over and over again all through the night it is not strange that they rise in the morning languid and dull instead of being refreshed and in high spirits. No one who is deprived of a sufficiency of fresh air can long remain efficient. Health is the cornerstone of success. I hear many nowadays talking of Eugenics. Eugenics was founded ten years ago by Sir Francis Galton, who defined it thus: "The study of agencies under control that may improve or impair the racial qualities of future generations, either physically or mentally." The University of London has adopted this definition, where a chair of Eugenics has been founded. This science is undoubtedly of the first importance, but what advantage is good birth if afterward life is poisoned with foul air? A dust-laden atmosphere is a germ-laden atmosphere, therefore physicians prescribe for tubercular convalescents conditions in which the air is 90% free from dust. However, the air of the city has been scientifically proven to be as pure as the air of the country. All that is necessary to secure proper lung food is plenty of it - houses so constructed that the air inside shall be free to go out and the air outside to come in. Air in a closed cage must be mischievous, and what are ill-ventilated rooms but vicious air cages, in which mischiefs of all sorts breed?

America professes to believe in publicity, and what is "publicity" but the open window and the open door? Practise this philosophy and it will be easy to keep on the sunny side of the street and to discourage the glooms. The joys fly in at open windows.

Notes

* I have never been a smoker and have always eschewed tobacco, cigarettes, etc.; though for a short while to oblige friends I occasionally accepted a cigarette, now I firmly refuse everything of the sort.

* Since writing the above, I have heard from an American lady that "progressive dinners" have recently been introduced by the idle and rich set of young people in New York. *The modus operandi* is that several dinners will, by arrangement, be given on a certain day, and the guests will go to each house alternately, eating one or two dishes only and remaining at the last house for fruit. I can hardly believe this, but my friend assures me it is a fact. It seems that eating is turned into play, and to appreciate the fun, I would like to be one of the actors.

* *The Living Temple* by J. H. Kellogg, pp. 282 et al. Published by Good Health Publishing Co., Battle Creek, Mich., U.S.A.

14

Theaters

The ideal of China is sincerity, but an actor is a pretender. He appears to be what he is not. Now our ancient wise men felt that pretense of any sort must have a dangerous reactionary influence on the character. If a man learns how to be a clever actor on the stage he may be a skilled deceiver in other walks of life. Moreover, no one to whom sincerity is as the gums are to the teeth, would wish to acquire the art of acting as though he were some one else. Hence actors in China have from ancient times been looked down upon. Actresses, until the last decade or so, were unknown in China, and a boy who became an actor could never afterward occupy any position of honor. He, his children and his grandchildren might be farmers, merchants or soldiers, but they could never be teachers, literary men or officials. The Chinese feeling for sincerity, amounting almost to worship, has caused the profession of an actor in China to be considered a very low one, and so until the new regime the actor was always debarred from attending any literary examination, and was also deprived of the privilege of obtaining official appointment; in fact he was considered an outcast of society. No respectable Chinese family would think of allowing their son to go on the stage. As a natural consequent the members of the Chinese stage have, as a rule, been men who were as much below the level of moral respectability as conventionalism had already adjudged them to be below the level of social respectability. Regard anyone as a mirror with a cracked face and he will soon justify your opinion of him. If the morals of Chinese actors will not bear investigation it is probably due to the social ostracism to which they have always been subjected. The same phenomenon may be seen in connection with Buddhism. As soon as Buddhism in China ceased to be a power the priests became a despised class and being despised they have often given occasion to others to despise them.

I am aware that quite a different view is held of the stage in America and Europe, and that actors and actresses are placed on an equal footing with other members of society. This does not, of course, mean that either America or Europe lays less stress on sincerity than China, but simply that we have developed in different ways. I have heard of the old "morality plays," I know that English drama, like the Egyptian, Greek, and Indian, had its origin in religion, but this alone will not explain the different attitude assumed toward actors in the West from that taken up in China. I am inclined to think that the reason why actors are not despised in the West as they are in China is because the West considers first the utility of pleasure, and the East the supremacy of sincerity. Here, as is so frequently the case, apparent differences are largely differences of emphasis. The West would seem to emphasize the beauty of the desire to please where Chinese consider the effect on character or business. The expensive dinners which no one eats and which I discussed in a previous chapter are an illustration. No one in China would spend money in this fashion excepting for some definite purpose.

We Chinese like to flatter, and to openly praise to their faces those whom we admire. Most Westerners, would, I think, please rather than admire; most men and women in America and Europe enjoy applause more than instruction. This recognition of the delicate pleasure of being able to please some one else naturally attracts quite a different type to the Western stage from the material usually found in Chinese dramatic companies, and in a society where everyone acknowledges the beauty of pleasing another, the position of the actor naturally becomes both envied and desirable. When therefore a man or woman succeeds on the European or American stage, he or she is looked up to and welcomed in fashionable society: Henry Irving had the *entree* to the highest society, and his portrait was always found among the notables. Newspapers published long notices of his stage performances, and when he died he received as great honors as England could give. During his lifetime he enjoyed the royal favor of Queen Victoria, who conferred a knighthood upon him. After his death his biography was published and read by thousands. All this is quite contrary to the spirit of the Chinese who, no matter how clever a man may be as an actor, can never forget that he is a pretender and that the cleverer he is the greater care exists for guarding one's self against his tricks.

Actresses are no less respected and honored in the West, whereas in China there are positively no respectable women on the stage. Yet in the West it is a common occurrence to hear of marriages of actresses to bankers, merchants, and millionaires. Even ballet-girls have become duchesses by marriage. The stage is considered a noble profession. Often, when a girl has a good voice, nothing will satisfy her but a stage career. A situation such as this is very difficult for a Chinese to analyze. The average Chinese woman lacks the imagination, the self-abandon, the courage which must be necessary before a girl can think of herself as standing alone in a bright light before a large audience waiting to see her dance or hear her sing. Chinese actresses were quite unknown until very recently, and the few that may be now found on the Chinese stage were nearly all of questionable character before they entered the theater. In the northern part of China some good Chinese women may be found in circuses, but these belong to the working class and take up the circus life with their husbands and brothers for a livelihood.

The actresses of the West are different. They are drawn to the stage for the sake of art; and it must be their splendid daring as much as their beauty which induces wealthy men, and even some of the nobility, to marry these women. Man loves courage and respects all who are brave enough to fight for their own. In a world where self-love (not selfishness) is highly esteemed, manhood, or the power of self-assertion, whether in man or woman, naturally becomes a fascinating virtue. No one likes to be colleague to a coward. The millionaires and others who have married actresses - and as actresses make plenty of money they are not likely to be willing to marry poor men - meet many women in society as beautiful as the women they see on the stage, but society women lack the supreme courage and daring of the stage girl. Thus, very often the pretty, though less educated, ballet-girl, wins the man whom her more refined and less self-assertive sister - the ordinary society girl - is sorry to lose.

The suffragettes are too intent just now on getting "Votes for Women" to listen to proposals of marriage, but when they succeed in obtaining universal suffrage I should think they would have little difficulty in obtaining brave husbands, for the suffragettes have courage. These women, however, are serious, and I do not think that men in the West, judging from what I have seen, like very serious wives. So perhaps after all the ballet-girl and actresses will have more chances in the marriage (I had almost written money) market than the suffragettes.

I may be mistaken in my theories. I have never had the opportunity of discussing the matter with a millionaire or an actress, nor have I talked about the stage with any of the ladies who make it their home, but unless it is their superb independence and their ability to throw off care and to act their part which attract men who are looking for wives, I cannot account for so many actresses marrying so well.

What, however, we may ask, is the object of the theater? Is it not amusement? But when a serious play ending tragically is put on the boards is that amusement? The feelings of the audience after witnessing such a play must be far from pleasant, and sometimes even moody; yet tragedies are popular, and many will pay a high price to see a well-known actor commit most objectionable imitation-crimes on the stage. A few weeks before this chapter was written a number of men of different nationalities were punished for being present at a cockfight in Shanghai. Mexican and Spanish bullfights would not be permitted in the United States, and yet it is a question whether the birds or the animals who take part in these fights really suffer very much. They are in a state of ferocious exaltation, and are more concerned about killing their opponents than about their own hurts. Soldiers have been seriously wounded without knowing anything about it until the excitement of the battle had died away. Why then forbid cockfighting or bull-baiting? They would be popular amusements if allowed. It is certain that animals that are driven long distances along dirty roads, cattle, sheep, and fowl that are cooped up for many weary hours in railway trucks, simply that they may reach a distant market and be slaughtered to gratify perverted human appetites, really suffer more than the cock or bull who may be killed or wounded in a fight with others of his own kind. What about the sufferings of pugilists who take part in the prize-fights, in which so many thousands in the United States delight? It cannot be pity, therefore, for the birds or beasts, which makes the authorities forbid cockfighting and bull-baiting. It must be that although these are exhibitions of courage and skill, the exhibition is degrading to the spectators and to those who urge the creatures to fight. But what is the difference, so far as the spectator is concerned, between watching a combat between animals or birds and following a vivid dramatization of cruelty on the stage? In the latter case the mental sufferings which are portrayed are frequently more harrowing than the details of any bull- or cockfight. Such representation, therefore, unless a very clear moral lesson or warning is emblazoned throughout the play, must have the effect of making actors, actresses and spectators less sympathetic with suffering. Familiarity breeds insensibility. What I have said of melodrama applies also, though in a lesser degree, to books, and should be a warning to parents to exercise proper supervision of their children's reading.

Far be it from me to disparage the work of the playwright; the plot is often well laid and the actors, especially the *primadonna*, execute their parts admirably. I am considering the matter, at the moment, from the view-point of a play-goer. What benefit does he receive from witnessing a tragedy? In his home and his office has he not enough to engage his serious attention, and to frequently worry his mind? Is it worth his while to dress and spend an evening watching a performance which, however skilfully played, will make him no happier than before? It is a characteristic of those who are fond of sensational plays that they do not mind watching the tragical ending of a hero or a heroine, and all for the sake of amusement. Young people and children are not likely to get good impressions from this sort of thing. It has even been said that murders have been committed by youngsters who had been taken by their parents to see a realistic melodrama. It is dangerous to allow young people of tender age to see such plays. The juvenile mind is not ripe enough to form correct judgments. Some time ago I read in one of the American papers that a boy had killed his father with a knife, on seeing him ill-treat his mother when in a state of intoxication. It appeared that the lad had witnessed a dramatic tragedy in a theater, and in killing his father considered he was doing a heroic act. He could, by the same rule, have been inspired to a noble act of self-sacrifice.

After all, the main question is, does a sensational play exercise a beneficial or a pernicious influence over the audience? If the reader will consider the matter impartially he should not have any difficulty in coming to a right conclusion.

Theatrical performances should afford amusement and excite mirth, as well as give instruction. People who visit theaters desire to be entertained and to pass the time pleasantly. Anything which excites mirth and laughter is always welcomed by an audience. But a serious piece from which humor has been excluded, is calculated, even when played with sympathetic feeling and skill, to create a sense of gravity among the spectators, which, to say the least, can hardly be restful to jaded nerves. Yet when composing his plays the playwright should never lose sight of the moral. Of course he has to pay attention to the arrangement of the different parts of the plot and the characters represented, but while it is important that each act and every scene should be harmoniously and properly set, and that the characters should be adapted to the piece as a whole, it is none the less important that a moral should be enforced by it. The practical lesson to be learned from the play should never be lost sight of. In Chinese plays the moral is always prominent. The villain is punished, virtue is rewarded, while the majority of the plays are historical. All healthy-minded people will desire to see a play end with virtue rewarded, and vice vanquished. Those who want it otherwise are unnatural and possess short views of life. Either in this life or in some other, each receives according to his deserts, and this lesson should always be taught by the play. Yet from all the clever dramas which have been written and acted on the Western stage from time to time what a very small percentage of moral lessons can be drawn, while too many of them have unfortunately been of an objectionable nature. Nearly everyone reads novels, especially the younger folk; to many of these a visit to a theater is like reading a novel, excepting that the performance makes everything more realistic. A piece with a good moral cannot therefore fail to make an excellent impression on the audience while at the same time affording them amusement.

I am somewhat surprised that the churches, ethical societies and reform associations in America do not more clearly appreciate the valuable aid they might receive from the stage. I have been told that some churches pay their singers more than their preachers, which shows that they have some idea of the value of good art. Why not go a step further and preach through a play? This does not mean that there should be no fun but that the moral should be well thrust home. I have heard of preachers who make jokes while preaching, so that it should not be so very difficult to act interesting sermons which would elevate, even if they did not amuse. People who went to church to see a theater would not expect the same entertainment as those who go to the theater simply for a laugh.

In China we do not expend as much energy as Americans and Europeans in trying to make other people good. We try to be good ourselves and believe that our good example, like a pure fragrance, will influence others to be likewise. We think practice is as good as precept, and, if I may say so without being supposed to be critical of a race different from my own, the thought has sometimes suggested itself to me that Americans are so intent on doing good to others, and on making others good, that they accomplish less than they would if their actions and intentions were less direct and obvious. I cannot here explain all I mean, but if my readers will study what Li Yu and Chuang Tsz have to say about "Spontaneity" and "Not Interfering," I think they will understand my thought. The theater, as I have already said, was in several countries religious in its origin; why not use it to elevate people indirectly? The ultimate effect, because more natural, might be better and truer than more direct persuasion. Pulpit appeals, I am given to understand, are sometimes very personal.

Since writing the above I have seen a newspaper notice of a dramatic performance in the Ethical Church, Queen's Road, Bayswater, London. The

Ethical Church believes "in everything that makes life sweet and human" and the management state that they believe - "the best trend of dramatic opinion today points not only to the transformation of theaters into centers of social enlightenment and moral elevation, but also to the transformation of the churches into centers for the imaginative presentation, by means of all the arts combined, of the deeper truths and meanings of life." Personally, I do not know anything about this society, but surely there is nothing out of harmony with Christianity in these professions, and I am glad to find here an alliance between the two greatest factors in the development of Western thought and culture - the church and the theater. The newspaper article to which I have referred was describing the "old morality play, Everyman" which had been performed in the church. The visitor who was somewhat critical, and apparently unused to seeing the theater in a church, wrote of the performance thus: "Both the music and the dressing of the play were perfect, and from the moment that Death entered clad in blue stuff with immense blue wings upon his shoulders, and the trump in his hand, and stopped Everyman, a gorgeous figure in crimson robes and jewelled turban, with the question, 'Who goes so gaily by?' the play was performed with an impressiveness that never faltered.

The heaviest burden, of course, falls on Everyman, and the artist who played this part seemed to me, though I am no dramatic critic, to have caught the atmosphere and the spirit of the play. His performance, indeed, was very wonderful from the moment when he offers Death a thousand boons if only the dread summons may be delayed, to that final tense scene, when, stripped of his outer robe, he says his closing prayers, hesitates for a moment to turn back, though the dread angel is there by his side, and then follows the beckoning hand of Good Deeds, a figure splendidly robed in flowing draperies of crimson and with a wonderfully expressive mobile face.

At the conclusion of the play Dr. Stanton Colt addressed a few words to the enthusiastic audience, Forsake thy pride, for it will profit thee nothing, he quoted, If we could but remember this more carefully and also the fact that nothing save our good deeds shall ever go with us into that other World, surely it would help us to a holier and better life. Earthly things have their place and

138

should have a due regard paid to them, but we must not forget the jewel of our souls.

I have, of course, heard of the "Passion Play" at Oberammergau in Germany where the life of Jesus Christ is periodically represented on the stage, but I say nothing about this, for, so far as I know, it is not performed in America, and I have not seen it; but I may note in passing that in China theaters are generally associated with the gods in the temples, and that the moral the play is meant to teach is always well driven home into the minds of the audience. We have not, however, ventured to introduce any of our sages to theater audiences.

The theater in China is a much simpler affair than in America. The residents in a locality unite and erect a large stage of bamboo and matting, the bamboo poles are tied with strips of rattan, and all the material of the stage, excepting the rattan, can be used over again when it is taken down. Most of the audience stand in front of the stage and in the open air, the theater generally being in front of the temple; and the play, which often occupies three or four days, is often performed in honor of the god's birthday. There is no curtain, and there are no stage accessories. The audience is thus enabled to concentrate its whole attention on the acting. Female parts are played by men, and everything is beautifully simple. There is no attempt to produce such elaborate effects as I have seen in the West, and of course nothing at all resembling the pantomime, which frequently requires mechanical arts. A newspaper paragraph caught my eye while thinking of this subject. I reproduce it:

The Century Theater in New York City has special apparatus for producing wind effects, thunder, and lightning simultaneously. The wind machine consists of a drum with slats which are rotated over an apron of corded silk, which produces the whistling sound of wind; the lightning is produced by powdered magnesium electrically ignited; thunder is simulated by rolling a thousand pounds of stone, junk and chain down a chute ending in an iron plate, followed by half-a-dozen cannon balls and supplemented by the deafening notes of a thunder drum.

Although, however, Chinese play-goers do not demand the expensive outfits and stage sceneries of the West, I must note here that not even on the American stage have I seen such gorgeous costumes, or robes of so rich a hue and displaying such glittering gold ornaments and graceful feathers, as I have seen on the simple Chinese stage I have just described. Western fashions are having a tendency in our ports and larger cities to modify some things that I have stated about Chinese theatrical performances, but the point I wish especially to impress on my readers is that theatrical performances in China, while amusing and interesting, are seldom melodramatic, and as I look back on my experiences in the United States, I cannot but think that the good people there are making a mistake in not utilizing the human natural love for excitement and the drama as a subsidiary moral investment. And, of course, all I have said of theaters applies with equal force to moving-picture shows.

15

Opera and Musical Entertainments

Opera is a form of entertainment which, though very popular in America and England, does not appeal to me. I know that those who are fond of music love to attend it, and that the boxes in an opera house are generally engaged by the fashionable set for the whole season beforehand. I have seen members of the "four hundred" in their boxes in a New York opera house; they have been distinguished by their magnificent toilettes and brilliant jewelry; but I have been thinking of the Chinese drama, which, like the old Greek play, is also based on music, and Chinese music with its soft and plaintive airs is a very different thing from the music of grand opera. Chinese music could not be represented on Western instruments, the intervals between the notes being different. Chinese singing is generally "recitative" accompanied by long notes, broken, or sudden chords from the orchestra. It differs widely from Western music, but its effects are wonderful. One of our writers has thus described music he once heard: "Softly, as the murmur of whispered words; now loud and soft together, like the patter of pearls and pearlets dropping upon a marble dish. Or liquid, like the warbling of the mango-bird in the bush; trickling like the streamlet on its downward course. And then like the torrent, stilled by the grip of frost, so for a moment was the music lulled, in a passion too deep for words." That this famous description of the effects of music which I have borrowed from Mr. Dyer Ball's *Things Chinese* is not exaggerated, anyone who knows China may confirm by personal observation of the keen enjoyment an unlearned, common day laborer will find in playing a single lute all by himself for hours beneath the moon on a warm summer evening, with no one listening but the trees and the flitting insects; but it requires a practised ear to appreciate singing and a good voice. On one occasion I went to an opera house in London to hear the world-renowned Madame Patti. The place was so crowded, and the atmosphere so close, that I felt very uncomfortable and I am ashamed to acknowledge that I had to leave before she had finished. If I had been educated to appreciate that sort of music no doubt I would have comprehended her singing better, and, however uncomfortable, I should no doubt have remained to the end of the entertainment.

While writing this chapter it happened that the following news from New York was published in the local papers in Shanghai. It should be interesting to my readers, especially to those who are lovers of music.

'Yellow music' will be the next novelty to startle and lure this blase town; amusement forecasters already see in the offing a Fall invasion of the mysterious Chinese airs which are now having such a vogue in London under the general term of 'yellow music'.

The time was when Americans and Occidentals in general laughed at Chinese music, but this was due to their own ignorance of its full import and to the fact that they heard only the dirges of a Chinese funeral procession or the brassy noises that feature a celestial festival. They did not have opportunity to be enthralled by the throaty, vibrant melodies - at once so lovingly seductive and harshly compelling - by which Chinese poets and lovers have revealed their thoughts and won their quest for centuries. The stirring tom-tom, if not the ragtime which sets the occidental capering today, was common to the Chinese three or four hundred years ago. They heard it from the wild Tartars and Mongols - heard it and rejected it, because it was primitive, untamed, and not to be compared with their own carefully controlled melodies. Mr. Emerson Whithorne, the famous British composer, who is an authority on oriental music, made this statement to the London music lovers last week:

'The popularity of Chinese music is still in its childhood. From now on it will grow rapidly. Chinese music has no literature, as we understand that term, but none can say that it has not most captivating melodies. To the artistic temperament, in particular, it appeals enormously, and well-known artists - musicians, painters, and so on - say that it affects them in quite an extraordinary way.'

Chinese music from an occidental standpoint has been unjustly described as "clashing cymbals, twanging guitars, harsh flageolets, and shrill flutes, ear-splitting and headache-producing to the foreigner." Such general condemnation shows deplorable ignorance. The writer had apparently never attended an official service in honor of Confucius, held biennially during the whole of the Ching dynasty at 3 A.M. The "stone chimes," consisting of sonorous stones varying in tone and hanging in frames, which were played on those solemn occasions, have a haunting melody such as can be heard nowhere else. China, I believe, is the only country that has produced music from stones. It is naturally gratifying to me to hear that Chinese airs are now having a vogue in London, and that they will soon be heard in New York. It will take some little time for Westerners to learn to listen intelligently to our melodies which, being always in unison, in one key and in one movement, are apt at first to sound as wearisome and monotonous as Madame Patti's complicated notes did to me, but when they understand them they will have found a new delight in life.

Although we Chinese do not divide our plays into comedies and tragedies there is frequently a good deal of humor on the Chinese stage; yet we have nothing in China corresponding to the popular musical comedy of the West. A musical comedy is really a series of vaudeville performances strung together by the feeblest of plots. The essence seems to be catchy songs, pretty dances, and comic dialogue. The plot is apparently immaterial, its only excuse for existence being to give a certain order of sequence to the aforesaid songs, dances, and dialogues. That, indeed, is the only object for the playwright's introducing any plot at all, hence he does not much care whether it is logical or even within the bounds of probability. The play-goers, I think, care even less. They go to hear the songs, see the dances, laugh at the dialogues, and indulge in frivolous frivolities; what do they want with a plot, much less a moral? Chinese vaudeville takes the form of clever tumbling tricks which I think are much preferable to the sensuous, curious, and self-revealing dances one sees in the West.

Although musical comedy, or, more properly speaking, musical farce, is becoming more and more popular in both Europe and America it is also becoming proportionately more farcical; although in many theaters it is staged as often as the more serious drama, in some having exclusive dominion; and although theater managers find that these plays draw bigger crowds and fill their houses better than any other, in the large cities running for over a year, I cannot help regarding this feature of theatrical life as so much theatrical chaos. It lacks culture, and is sometimes both bizarre and neurotic. I do not object to patter, smart give and take, in which the comical angles of life are exposed, if it is brilliant; neither have I anything to say against light comedy in which the ridiculous side of things is portrayed. This sort of entertainment may help men who have spent a busy day, crowded with anxious moments, and weighted with serious responsibilities, but exhibitions which make men on their way home talk not of art, or of music, or of wit, but of "the little girl who wore a little black net" are distinctly to be condemned. Even the class who think it waste of time to think, and who go to the theater only to "laugh awfully," are not helped by this sort of entertainment. Such songs as the following, which I have culled from the 'Play Pictorial,' a monthly published in London, must in time pall the taste of even the shallow-minded.

> Can't you spare a glance?
> Have we got a chance?
> You've got a knowing pair of eyes;
> When it's 2 to 1
> It isn't much fun,

This is what she soon replies:

Oh, won't you buy a race-card,
And take a tip from me?
If you want to find a winner,
It's easy as can be
When the Cupid stakes are starting,
Your heads are all awhirl,
And my tip today
Is a bit each way
On the race-card girl.

Yet this, apparently, is the sort of thing which appeals to the modern American who wants amusement of the lightest kind, amusement which appeals to the eye and ear with the lightest possible tax on his already over-burdened brain. He certainly cannot complain that his wishes have not been faithfully fulfilled. It may be due to my ignorance of English, but the song I have just quoted seems to me silly, and I do not think any "ragtime music" could make it worth singing. Of course many songs and plays in the music halls are such as afford innocent mirth, but it has to be confessed that there are other things of a different type which it is not wise for respectable families to take the young to see. I would not like to say all I think of this feature of Western civilization, but I may quote an Englishman without giving offense. Writing in the 'Metropolitan Magazine', Louis Sherwin says:

There is not a doubt that the so-called 'high-brow dancer' has had a lot to do with the bare-legged epidemic that rages upon the comic-opera stage today. Nothing could be further removed from musical comedy than the art of such women as Isadora Duncan and Maude Allen. To inform Miss Duncan that she has been the means of making nudity popular in musical farce would beyond question incur the lady's very reasonable wrath. But it is none the less true. When the bare-legged classic dancer made her appearance in opera houses, and on concert platforms with symphony orchestras, it was the cue for every chorus girl with an ambition to undress in public. First of all we had a plague of

Salomes. Then the musical comedy producers, following their usual custom of religiously avoiding anything original, began to send the pony ballets and soubrettes on the stages without their hosiery and with their knees clad in nothing but a coat of whitewash (sometimes they even forgot to put on the whitewash, and then the sight was horrible). The human form divine, with few exceptions, is a devilish spectacle unless it is properly made up. Some twenty years from now managers will discover what audiences found out months ago, that a chorus girl's bare leg is infinitely less beautiful than the same leg when duly disguised by petticoats and things.

16

Conjuring and Circuses

After what I have said as to the position of the actor in China my readers will not be surprised at my saying that the performance of a conjuror should not be encouraged. What pleasure can there be in being tricked? It may be a great display of dexterity to turn water into wine, to seem to cut off a person's head, to appear to swallow swords, to escape from locked handcuffs, and to perform the various cabinet tricks, but cleverness does not alter the fact that after all it is only deception cunningly contrived and performed in such a way as to evade discovery. It appears right to many because it is called "*legerdemain*" and "conjuring" but in reality it is exactly the same thing as that by which the successful card-sharper strips his victims, viz. such quickness of hand that the eye is deceived. Should we encourage such artful devices? History tells many stories as to the way in which people have been kept in superstitious bondage by illusions and magic, and if it be now held to be right to deceive for fun how can it be held to have been wrong to deceive for religion? Those who made the people believe through practising deception doubtless believed the trick to be less harmful than unbelief. I contend, therefore, that people who go to see conjuring performances derive no good from them, but that, on the contrary, they are apt to be impressed with the idea that to practise deception is to show praiseworthy skill. It is strange how many people pay money to others to deceive them. More than ever before, people today actually enjoy being cheated. If the tricks were clumsily devised and easily detected there would be no attraction, but the cleverer and more puzzling the trick the more eagerly people flock to see it.

Christian preachers and moralists could do well to take up this matter and discourage people from frequenting the exhibitions of tricksters. There are doubtless many laws in nature yet undiscovered, and a few persons undoubtedly possess abnormal powers. This makes the cultivation of the love of trickery the more dangerous. It prevents the truth from being perceived. It enables charlatans to find dupes, and causes the real magician to be applauded as a legerdemainist. This is what the New Testament tells us happened in the case of Jesus Christ. His miracles failed to convince because the people had for a long time loved those who could deceive them cleverly. The people said to him, "Thou hast a devil," and others warned them after his death saying, "That deceiver said while he was yet alive 'After three days I will rise again.' " When people are taught not only to marvel at the marvelous but to be indifferent to its falsehoods they lose the power of discrimination, and are apt to take the true for the false, the real for the unreal.

For an evening's healthy enjoyment I believe a circus is as good a place as can be found anywhere. The air there is not close and vitiated as in a theater; you can spend two or three hours comfortably without inhaling noxious atmospheres. It is interesting to note that the circus is perhaps the only form of ancient entertainment which has retained something of its pristine simplicity. Today, as in the old Roman circuses, tiers of seats run round the course, which in the larger circuses is still in the form of an ellipse, with its vertical axis, where the horses and performers enter, cut away. But the modern world has nothing in this connection to compare with the Circus Maximus of Rome, which, according to Pliny, held a quarter of a million spectators. It is singular, however, that while the old Roman circuses were held in permanent buildings, modern circuses are mostly travelling exhibitions in temporary erections. In some respects the entertainment offered has degenerated with the change, for we have today nothing in the circus to correspond to the thrilling chariot races in which the old Romans delighted. I wonder that in these days of restless search for novelties some one does not re-introduce the Roman chariot race under the old conditions, and with a reproduction of the old surroundings. It would be as interesting and as exciting as, and certainly less dangerous than, polo played in automobiles, which I understand is one of the latest fads in the West. A modern horse-race, with its skill, daring and picturesqueness, is the only modern entertainment comparable to the gorgeous races of the Romans.

The exhibition of skillful feats of horsemanship and acrobatic displays by juvenile actors, rope-dancing, high vaulting and other daring gymnastic feats seen in any of our present-day circuses are interesting, but not new. The Romans had many clever tight-rope walkers, and I do not think they used the long pole loaded at the ends to enable them to maintain their equilibrium, as do some later performers. Japanese tumblers are very popular and some of their tricks clever, but I think the Western public would find Chinese acrobats a pleasant diversion. With practice, it would seem as if when taken in hand during its supple years there is nothing that cannot be done with the human body. Sometimes it almost appears as if it were boneless, so well are people able by practice to make use of their limbs to accomplish feats which astonish ordinary persons whose limbs are less pliable.

The trapeze gives opportunity for the display of very clever exhibition, of strength and agility; at first sight the gymnast would appear to be flying from one cross-bar to the other, and when watching such flights I have asked myself: "If a person can do that, why cannot he fly?" Perhaps human beings will some day be seen flying about in the air like birds. It only requires an extension of the trapeze "stunt." Travelling in the air by means of airships or aeroplanes is tame sport in comparison with bird-like flights, whether with or without artificial wings.

There are many advantages in being able to travel in the air. One is a clear and pure atmosphere such as cannot be obtained in a railway car, or in a cabin on board a ship; another is the opportunity afforded of looking down on this earth, seeing it as in a panorama, with the people looking like ants. Such an experience must broaden the mental outlook of the privileged spectator, and enable him to guess how fragmentary and perverted must be our restricted view of things in general. There is, however, danger of using such opportunities for selfish and mischievous purposes. A wicked man might throw a bomb or do some other wicked nonsense just as some one else, who really sees things as they are and not as they seem to be, might employ his superior knowledge to benefit himself and injure his fellows; but the mention of the trapeze and its bird-like performers has diverted me from my theme.

I suppose that a reference to the circus would be incomplete which overlooked the clowns, those poor survivals of a professional class of jesters who played what appears to have been a necessary part in society in ruder days, when amusements were less refined and less numerous. The Chinese have never felt the need of professional foolers, and I cannot say that I admire the circus clown, but the intelligence which careful training develops in the horse, the dog, etc., interests me a good deal. An instance of this came under my own observation during a recent visit to Shanghai of "Fillis' Circus." Mr. Fillis had a mare which for many years had acted the part of the horse of a highway robber. The robber, flying from his enemies, urges the animal beyond its strength, and the scene culminated with the dying horse being carried from the arena to the great grief of its master. When this entertainment was given in Shanghai this horse - "Black Bess" - fell sick. A tonic was administered in the shape of the lively tune which the band always played as she was about to enter the arena and play her part as the highwayman's mare. The animal made pitiable attempts to rise, and her inability to do so apparently suggested to the intelligent creature the dying scene she had so often played. She lay down and relaxed, prepared to die in reality. The attendants, ignorant of the manner in which the horse had let herself go, tried to lift her, but in her relaxed condition her bowels split - Black Bess had acted her part for the last time.

17

Sports

Perhaps in nothing do the Chinese differ from their Western friends in the matter of amusements more than in regard to sports. The Chinese would never think of assembling in thousands just to see a game played. We are not modernized enough to care to spend half a day watching others play. When we are tired of work we like to do our own playing. Our national game is the shuttlecock, which we toss from one to another over our shoulders, hitting the shuttlecock with the flat soles of the shoes we are wearing. Sometimes we hit with one part of the foot, sometimes with another, according to the rules of the game. This, like kite-flying, is a great amusement among men and boys.

We have nothing corresponding to tennis and other Western ball games, nor, indeed, any game in which the opposite sexes join. Archery was a health-giving exercise of which modern ideas of war robbed us. The same baneful influence has caused the old-fashioned healthful gymnastic exercises with heavy weights to be discarded. I have seen young men on board ocean-going steamers throwing heavy bags of sand to one another as a pastime. This, though excellent practice, hardly equals our ancient athletic feats with the bow or the heavy weight. Western sports have been introduced into some mission and other schools in China, but I much doubt if they will ever be really popular among my people. They are too violent, and, from the oriental standpoint, lacking in dignity. Yet, when Chinese residing abroad do take up Western athletic sports they prove themselves the equals of all competitors, as witness their success in the Manila Olympiad, and the name the baseball players from the Hawaiian Islands Chinese University made for themselves when they visited America. Nevertheless, were the average Chinese told that many people buy the daily paper in the West simply to see the result of some game, and that a sporting journalism flourishes there, i.e., papers devoted entirely to sport, they would regard the statement as itself a pleasant sport. Personally, I think we might learn much from the West in regard to sports. They certainly increase the physical and mental faculties, and for this reason, if for no other, deserve to be warmly supported. China suffers because her youths have never been trained to team-work. We should be a more united people if as boys and young men we learned to take part in games which took the form of a contest, in which, while each contestant does his best for his own side, the winning or losing of the game is not considered so important as the pleasure of the exercise. I think a great deal of the manliness which I have admired in the West must be attributed to the natural love of healthy sport for sport's sake. Games honestly and fairly played inculcate the virtues of honor, candidness, and chivalry, of which America has produced many worthy specimens. When one side is defeated the winner does not exult over his defeated opponents but attributes his victory to an accident; I have seen the defeated crew in a boat race applauding their winning opponents. It is a noble example for the defeated contestants to give credit to and to applaud the winner, an example which I hope will be followed by my countrymen.

As an ardent believer in the natural, healthy and compassionate life I was interested to find in the Encyclopaedia Britannica how frequently vegetarians have been winners in athletic sports. They won the Berlin to Dresden walking match, a distance of 125 miles, the Carwardine Cup (100 miles) and Dibble Shield (6 hours) cycling races (1901–2), the amateur championship of England in tennis (four successive years up to 1902) and racquets (1902), the cycling championship of India (three years), half-mile running championship of Scotland (1896), world's amateur cycle records for all times from four hours to thirteen hours (1902), 100 miles championship Yorkshire Road Club (1899, 1901), tennis gold medal (five times). I have not access to later statistics on this subject but I know that it is the reverse of truth to say, as Professor Gautier, of the *Sarbonne*, a Catholic foundation in Paris, recently said, that vegetarians "suffer from lack of energy and weakened will power." The above facts disprove it, and as against Prof. Gautier, I quote Dr. J. H. Kellogg, the eminent physician and Superintendent of Battle Creek Sanitarium in Michigan, U.S.A., who has been a strict vegetarian for many years and who, though over sixty years of age, is as strong and vigorous as a man of forty; he told me that he worked sixteen hours daily without the least fatigue. Mrs. Annie Besant, President of the Theosophical Society, is another example. I am credibly informed that she has been a vegetarian for at least thirty-five years and that it is doubtful if any flesh-eater who is sixty-five can equal her in energy. Whatever else vegetarians may lack they are not lacking in powers of endurance.

It is needless for me to say that hunting, or, as it is called, "sport", is entirely opposed to my idea of the fitness of things. I do not see why it should not be as interesting to shoot at "clay pigeons" as to kill living birds; and why moving targets are not as suitable a recreation as running animals. "The pleasures of the chase" are no doubt fascinating, but when one remembers that these so-called pleasures are memories we have brought with us from the time when we were savages and hunted for the sake of food, no one can be proud of still possessing such tastes. To say that hunters today only kill to eat would be denied indignantly by every true sportsman. That the quarry is sometimes eaten afterward is but an incident in the game; the splendid outdoor exercise which the hunt provides can easily be found in other ways without inflicting the fear, distress, and pain which the hunted animals endure. It is a sad commentary on the stage at which humanity still is that even royalty, to whom we look for virtuous examples, seldom misses an opportunity to hunt. When a man has a strong hobby he is unable to see its evil side even though in other respects he may be humane and kind-hearted. Thus the sorry spectacle is presented of highly civilized and humane people displaying their courage by hunting and attacking wild animals, not only in their own native country but in foreign lands as well. Such personages are, I regret to have to add, not unknown in the United States.

The fact that hunting has been followed from time immemorial, that the ancient Egyptians, Assyrians, and Babylonians indulged in this pastime, does not make it any more suitable an occupation for us today. The good qualities of temper and patience which hunting demands are equally well developed by athletic sports. I understand that a good hunting establishment will cost as much as $10,000 (2,000 pounds) a year. Surely those who can afford so much on luxuries could find a more refined amusement in yachting and similar recreations. To sail a yacht successfully in half a gale of wind, is, I should imagine, more venturesome, more exciting, and a pastime requiring a manifestation of more of the qualities of daring, than shooting a frightened animal from the safe retreat of the saddle of a trusty horse; and not even the hunt of the wild beast can equal in true sportsmanship a contest with the wind and the waves, for it is only occasionally that a beast shows fight because he is wounded, and even then man is well protected by his gun; but whether yachting or swimming the sportsman's attitude of watchfulness is uninterrupted. I fancy it is convention and custom, rather than conviction of the superiority of the sport, that has given hunting its pre-eminence. It is on record that four thousand years ago the ancient emperors of China started periodically on hunting expeditions. They thus sought relief from the monotony of life in those days; in the days of the Stuarts, in England, royalty found pleasure in shows which were childish and even immoral. Of course in barbarous countries all savages used to hunt for food. For them hunting was an economic necessity, and it is no slander to say that the modern hunt is a relic of barbarism. It is, indeed, a matter of surprise to me that this cruel practice has not ceased, but still exists in this twentieth century. It goes without saying that hunting means killing the defenseless, inflicting misery and death on the helpless; even if it be admitted that there is some justification for killing a ferocious and dangerous animal, why should we take pleasure in hunting and killing the fox, the deer, the hare, the otter, and similar creatures? People who hunt boast of their bravery and fearlessness, and to show their intrepidity and excellent shooting they go to the wilderness and other countries to carry on their "sport." I admire their fearless courage but I am compelled to express my opinion that such actions are not consistent with those of a good-hearted humane gentleman.

Still less excuse is there for the practice of shooting. What right have we to wantonly kill these harmless and defenseless birds flying in the air? I once watched pigeon shooting at a famous watering place, the poor birds were allowed to fly from the trap-holes simply that they might be ruthlessly killed or maimed. That was wanton cruelty; to reprobate too strongly such revolting barbarity is almost impossible. I am glad to say that such cruel practices did not come under my observation during my residence in the States, and I hope that they are not American vices but are prohibited by law. No country, with the least claim to civilization, should allow such things, and our descendants will be astonished that people calling themselves civilized should have indulged in such wholesale and gratuitous atrocities. When people allow animals to be murdered - for it is nothing but murder - for the sake of sport, they ought not to be surprised that men are murdered by criminals for reasons which seem to them good and sufficient. An animal has as much right to its life as man has to his. Both may be called upon to sacrifice life for the sake of some greater good to a greater number, but by what manner of reasoning can killing for killing's sake be justified? Does the superior cunning and intellect of man warrant his taking life for fun? Then, should a race superior to humanity ever appear on the earth, man would have no just cause of complaint if he were killed off for its amusement. There formerly existed in India a "well-organized confederacy of professional assassins" called Thugs, who worshipped the goddess Kali with human lives. They murdered according to "rigidly prescribed forms" and for religious reasons. The English, when they came into power in India, naturally took vigorous measures to stamp out Thuggeeism; but from a higher point of view than our own little selves, is there after all so much difference between the ordinary sportsman and the fanatic Thuggee? If there be, the balance is rather in favor of the latter, for the Thug at least had the sanction of religion, while the hunter has

155

nothing to excuse his cruelty beyond the lust of killing. I do not understand why the humane societies, such as "The Society for the Prevention of Cruelty to Animals," are so supine in regard to these practices. The Chinese are frequently accused of being cruel to animals, but I think that those who are living in glass houses should not throw stones.

In this connection I would remark that birds are shot not only for pleasure and for their flesh, but in some cases for their plumage, and women who wear hats adorned with birds' feathers, do, though indirectly, encourage the slaughter of the innocent. Once a Chinese was arrested by the police in Hong Kong for cruelty to a rat. It appeared that the rat had committed great havoc in his household, stealing and damaging various articles of food; when at last it was caught the man nailed its feet to a board, as a warning to other rats. For this he was brought before the English Magistrate, who imposed a penalty of ten dollars. He was astonished, and pleaded that the rat deserved death, on account of the serious havoc committed in his house. The Magistrate told him that he ought to have instantly killed the rat, and not to have tortured it. The amazed offender paid his fine, but murmured that he did not see the justice of the British Court in not allowing him to punish the rat as he chose, while foreigners in China were allowed the privilege of shooting innocent birds without molestation. I must confess, people are not always consistent.

The Peace Societies should take up this matter, for hunting is an imitation of war and an apprenticeship to it. It certainly can find no justification in any of the great world religions, and not even the British, or the Germans, who idolize soldiers, would immortalize a man simply because he was a hunter. From whatever point the subject be viewed it seems undeniable that hunting is only a survival of savagery.

Notes

* E. B., 9th ed., vol. 33, p. 649.